EQUIDO

The Path of Least Resistance

Morag Higgins & Mark Higgins

Fisher King Publishing

EQUIDO - THE PATH OF LEAST RESISTANCE

Fisher King Publishing Ltd,
The Studio,
Arthington Lane,
Pool in Wharfedale,
LS21 1JZ,
England.

www.fisherkingpublishing.co.uk

ISBN 978-1-910406-69-4

DEDICATION

We would like to dedicate this book to the memories of:

James Arthur Earnshaw Colquhoun

James Iain Colquhoun

Without whom this journey would never have been started.

THANK YOU

We would like to offer a special thank you to all of the clients and owners who allowed us to work with their horses. In particular Alison Masterson and her beautiful horse Beth who partnered Mark in most of the technical photographs.

We would also like to thank:-

Douglas Keegan of Keegan Photography for his outstanding contribution without which this book would be very thin!

Sky View Video (Scotland) for their amazing drone photography and video.

Rick Armstrong of Fisher King Publishing for his constant support and belief in our equestrian work.

Andrea Hibbert Equine Shiatsu for her fabulous work.

Vicky Devlin Masterson®Method for her fabulous work.

Stuart Alexander Armstrong FWCF

Chris Armstrong BVMS MRCVS Clyde Veterinary Group

All of our wonderful staff and instructors who have worked tirelessly in the background.

Gerry Burns from AW Jenkins arena surfaces

"This book is a must for any human who wants a greater bond, a greater understanding and a greater way of being with their horse. Providing clear knowledge and understanding to allow us humans to look at our role and what we bring to our equine relationship not only in the saddle but on the ground. Equido provides a clear path to enhance our relationship with our treasured equines. I truly believe if you want to gain insight, knowledge and understanding then this book is the one - written by specialists who are leading the way in the equine world!"

Margaret Rae - Learning & Development, Training & Coaching Consultant

"This book brings horse and human together as one and helps the reader understand how both are equal and how understanding our horse helps us achieve our goals."

Andrea Hibbert - Shiatsu Practitioner

"Mark and Morag are skilled, dedicated and 'listen' to the horses point of view. If horses could smile they would!"

Vicky Devlin - Masterson Method Practitioner

"I have been looking for a different approach to take in my work with remedial horses and I am extremely lucky to have found Equido. It has taken me to a deeper understanding of our Equine companions. A very useful guide to take with you on your journey as a horseman or woman."

Antoine Ruault - Equido Level 4 Student

"We can sometimes unwittingly place obstacles in the paths of our horses causing confusion and frustration for all concerned. For the sake of the horse, we must strive to do better – to be better – this is at the very heart of Mark and Morag's work."

Laura Manby - Equido Level 3 Student

Contents

Introduction   1

Foreword   3

Chapter 1 - Who are we?   7

Chapter 2 - Teaching   12

Chapter 3 - Bodywork   16

Chapter 4 - Assessing Us   43

Chapter 5 - Assessing the Horse   47

Chapter 6 - Toolbox   71

Chapter 7 - Liberty Work   240

Chapter 8 - Loading   260

Chapter 9 - Finding Solutions   290

Chapter 10 - Something to Think About   322

Suggested Reading and Websites   327

Charities   328

Disclaimer   329

INTRODUCTION

The primary reason for the development of Equido® is to educate people, from basic to advanced horsemanship, in a method that is sympathetic to the needs of the horse. Equido® has been accredited by LANTRA for over ten years and in that time there have been over 500 students who have studied the system. The premise for writing this book is to show people another perspective in working with horses.

Within these pages you will see vets, farriers, bodyworkers and trainers going about their day-to-day work as a result some of the pictures show horses coming in from the field. What you see is an honest representation of work carried out on a yard. We also wanted to show that it is not just the trainer who is involved with the horse but a team of highly skilled equestrian professionals.

In reading this book our hope is that you find information that is beneficial to you and your horse and perhaps this will be the start of your journey of discovery along the path of least resistance.

"Some of our greatest teachers have four legs"
Mark Higgins

FOREWORD

It is my love of horses that has, to date, provided me with an amazing journey, and whilst there have been challenges there have been wonderful rewards. One of the most valued I hold dear is being introduced to Morag and Mark Higgins of Equido® Horsemanship. A chance introduction which has changed my life and that of my horse's for the better! I consider myself lucky to have made such great friends and associates. And now I have been given one of the greatest honours' in writing this foreword for a publication that I believe is a must read for every horse owner who believes in building an everlasting, ever evolving bond with their horse.

Mark brings a real depth of connection, energy and understanding to his horsemanship and through his writing you will feel the passion he has for his work. Morag is uncomplicated, open and honest, not only is she an accomplished rider, a true horse behaviourist with a wealth of expertise in horse care and management to share and to educate horse owners and riders at all levels, she is also an author of science fiction. She has fabulous stories to tell!

Together Morag and Mark have designed and developed Equido® a unique and comprehensive training methodology and system. They are outstanding specialists, trainers and educators for the 21st Century.

What I love most about this book is that it is much, much more than a source of knowledge, it is inspiring, innovative and deeply focused on the human/horse relationship. Morag and Mark have the ability to closely read a horse's body-language, the minimal cues, and the herd mentality. Their expertise and wisdom clearly stands out, and this book is full of their learnings, skills, knowledge and expertise. Written clearly open, honest with passion and from the heart focusing on the horse and the human elements.

This book sets out to inform the owner/rider of the responsibility they bring with them in building a positive relationship with their horse. So many equine publications focus on how to get this or that from your horse,

and the attention is heavily on 'changing' the personality of the horse or worst still the introduction to the mystical carrot, gimmick or gadget that will supposedly enhance your interaction with your horse! Not here, in this book you will find a proven methodology which is easy to read, digest and learn.

Rest assured as you go through the pages here you will understand the importance of what you bring to the partnership. As we increase our understanding of how we communicate with our horse so we reach a new level of understanding of ourselves. Consider this book as a guide to your learning style, your thought processes, and your interactions not only in your relationship with your horse but across all areas of your life.

As a psychotherapist, coach and educator I believe The Path of Least Resistance is a natural selection for anyone who wants to build a firm foundation in the development of an everlasting bond with their horse. One thing is for sure, when you put into practice the teaching within this book you will increase your ability to positively enhance the outcomes for all.

Margaret Rae
Inverkip, Inverclyde, Scotland

"Horses are very keen on body language,
and what I refer to as "presence" and expression.
They know quite a bit about you before you ever get to them.
They can read things about you clear across the arena."
Buck Brannaman

Chapter One – Who are we?

Morag Higgins - WESI MRPCH HNCES BHSAI

Morag Higgins has (along with her husband Mark) developed an independent system that builds on the principles of good horsemanship.

Morag has been riding now for over forty years and teaching for most of that time. Having had the privilege to have known and worked with many horses in her career she always felt that there was something new to learn from every one of them. It was only recently that she found a path that allowed her to truly listen to what they were saying.

Her riding career has been very varied, having participated in several disciplines such as jumping, dressage, one day eventing, showing and now western riding. Looking back at the horses she has known Morag feels humble to have been taught by them.

Initially her training was traditional, she also was a traditional trainer and rider. This held her in good stead for the years of competition in strict disciplines, but through it all she felt she was always seeking more.

Over the years Morag learned so much from the troubled horses she was working with and began to build on and expand the techniques that had been shown to her. The moment of revelation came when, in 2005, Morag had the good fortune to ride on a clinic with top American trainer Mark Rashid. Truly inspired, as Mark Rashid is not only an exceptional horseman but human being as well as a fellow Martial Artist, Morag instantly understood his ethos, which steered her down the path of least resistance.

At times Morag has had to let go of previous beliefs and open her mind to new and, what seemed like, radical ideas. However, she can honestly say that by following this way of thinking her life has changed and she has changed as a person. Morag has become a much better rider, more receptive and responsive to the horses she rides and she can now listen to what they say and feel.

Along with her team of instructors they have developed a complete system that builds on those principles and philosophy as taught by Mark Rashid, this system is Equido®. It is easy to learn and available to all who wish to expand their knowledge and grow in their horsemanship skills. This course has been endorsed by LANTRA.

Mark Higgins - EQUIDO LEVEL 4

Mark has been working with horses for twenty years and is one of the co-writers of Equido®. As a Level 4 Instructor he currently specializes in Groundwork and teaches both privately and at clinics throughout the UK and Europe.

"People will forget what you have said.
People will forget what you did.
But people will never forget how you made them feel."
Unknown

Having suffered abuse as a child, Mark found that he had an instant connection with horses, especially ones that have been mentally and physically scarred. Like his wife, Morag, Mark has studied with Mark Rashid and also Crissi McDonald, finding inspiration in their guidance. Mark is also a student of The Masterson Method® and is training towards his practitioner's certification.

He now heads Equido® Horsemanship Ltd and plays an integral part in the training of external and internal client horses that are looking to find a softer feel in their work. He has trained in the Martial Arts of Aikido and Ninjutsu and incorporates the philosophy of timing, energy and feel in his groundwork sessions.

Human Learning and Development

I hear the coined phrase 'self-development' a lot these days. We humans are learning all the time both on a conscious and an unconscious level. We continually learn and are ever evolving. All learning includes self-development. This can include learning to behave differently, learning to think differently, and learning to feel differently. In this ever changing world we are continuously adapting and adopting to change.

We often hear people referring to learning as gaining skills and knowledge through hands on experience, or being taught something, studying a topic or through education. Is this learning? Or is this the result of learning? It is quite clearly the result. If we want to know how we learn then we need to look at the process, and how we operate. What makes us tick.

Understanding how we learn is helpful in assisting us to make our learning as effective as possible and to help address any set-backs that may happen along the path of our journey.

That said, I would also add one more to the list and that is what psychologists describe as being in 'flow'.

This concept came from the work of psychologist Mihaly Csikszentmihalyi and is referred to when we are fully engaged, fully absorbed and focused on an activity to the exclusion of everything else. We are completely engrossed in what we are doing, fully motivated in the moment, in the task. If you are fully in the zone, and you feel positive and emotionally driven by what you are doing you are more likely to be in 'flow'. When individuals experience flow they comment that there is also a feel good factor, a feeling of sheer delight whilst carrying out the task or work.

As well as being aware of the learning process it is also important to understand the different learning styles. We all have our own learning style which directly correlates with our values and beliefs. Our learning style links directly with how we make sense of our own world. Our interpretation of the world around us is through our five senses: Visual; Aural; Kinesthetic: Olfactory; Gustatory. However, commonly within learning and education environments the VAK model is referred to as the learners preferred style, and although you may have a preferred learning style you will move between the styles detailed below:

Visual learners like diagrams, charts, flow diagrams and symbols, a very graphic learner. But beware this doesn't include photographs or movies or PowerPoint. However, they do like designs and a variety of formats to highlight information.

Aural/Auditory learners preferred method is information that is spoken or heard – learning from lectures, radio, and group discussion. They also like talking out loud as well unto themselves. They like to sort by speaking - the opportunity to say information again. Saying it in their own way – in their own words.

Read/write learners preferred method is information in words, text based – reading and writing. Often the learner utilises PowerPoint, the internet, the use of lists and notes. They especially like reports, written words, written tasks and essays.

Kinesthetic learners prefer a hands-on approach, combining experience and practice – both simulated and real. This can include demonstrations, simulations, videos and movies of 'real' things, as well as case studies, practice and application. A very hands on approach - if it can be grasped, held, or felt it is probably to be included here. Can be known as learning by doing.

Your Mind Impacts on your Behaviour!

Coming from a cognitive behaviourist view point, what we see and read, what we hear and say, what we feel and do, what we smell and what we taste creates mental maps in our mind creating files of our experience to enable us to make sense of our world. For example, a group of friends go to a party and although they are all at the party together each individual's experience of the party may differ.

Cognitive behaviour continues to develop with advancements in neuroscience. We make mind-body connections all the time both consciously and unconsciously through our thought processes. Our thoughts create feelings which then create our behaviours and then actions the results that we get from that thought in the mind.

If you want to change your behaviour you need to change your thoughts. There are vast numbers of evidence-based therapies and approaches that can help you with this, for example cognitive behavioural therapy, mindfulness, yoga, and clinical hypnotherapy.

Being aware of 'self' is hugely important if we want to help others and make better connections in our relationships with others or with our horses. Before running head-long into helping others or your horses, first make time for you. Set to work on you before you work on anyone else and that includes your horse.

"The 'point of resistance' in our partner (whether horse or human) is the spot at which the partner is thinking about resisting, but hasn't done so yet. Often this is an area so small that reaching it is like balancing on the blade of a very sharp knife. It is the point at which, simultaneously, all things are available, and nothing is available. Moving just a hair one way or another will either get us everything we are looking for or nothing at all. Finding that edge is the path to great horsemanship, working the edge is the path to mastery."
Mark Rashid

Chapter Three – Bodywork

Masterson Method®

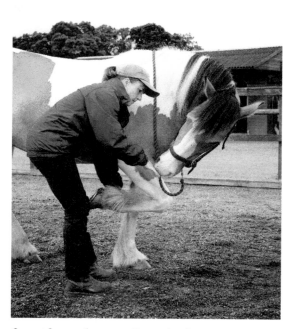

Horses can have difficulties in training for many reasons, one thing that should be ruled out is physical tension or pain. Regular bodywork can help identify and eventually eliminate many of the problems that could be causing training issues. For example, a horse that has tension in the poll may find it difficult to work with any collected movements.

The Masterson Method® is an integrated, multi-modality method of equine massage. It is a unique, interactive form of equine massage in which you learn to recognize and use the responses of the horse to your touch to find and release accumulated tension in key junctions of the body that most affect performance. In contrast to most traditional modalities, it enables the horse to actively participate in the process of releasing tension. It is something you do *with* the horse, rather than *to* the horse. This participation and interaction are what makes the method fascinating for those who use it. In fact, if you do not allow the horse to participate, it does not work!

When practicing equine massage and bodywork on horses, we can only achieve good results if the horse remains cooperative and relaxed. This can be challenging. In nature, the horse's first survival response to intrusion is to flee. When we are handling the horse, it normally doesn't have that option. It falls back to its second survival response; to guard, push against, or brace. This can happen either externally or internally. You can stay under the radar of this "survival response" by applying pressure to the horse lightly enough and slowly enough and therefore bypass this internal bracing or guarding response. The Masterson Method® enables you to access that part of the horse's nervous system that will yield, or release tension.

Achieving release: How subtle responses from the horse lead to release of tension. As a prey animal, the horse will attempt to always appear strong. If the horse shows signs of pain or weakness it will be the one first noticed by the predator, or may be left behind by the herd. Every horse will guard against showing signs of pain, weakness, lameness in the body. That is why it can be so difficult to evaluate lameness in a horse. By applying the Masterson Method® you can access that part of the horse's nervous system that will give you certain signs that tell you where tension is being held in the body, and when it is being released. If

you use the correct level of touch or pressure, and follow what the horse's own body is telling you, it will release the tension it is holding onto.

Certain areas of the horse's body accumulate stress and tension that affect mobility, comfort, attitude and performance. This can come from any number of areas including feet, saddle, teeth, conformation, lameness or just plain work. When the tension is released you see immediate improvement in mobility, comfort, attitude and performance.

The Masterson Method® focuses on releasing tension in key junctions of the body that most affect performance such as the poll, neck/shoulder/withers junction, and sacro/lumbar junction.

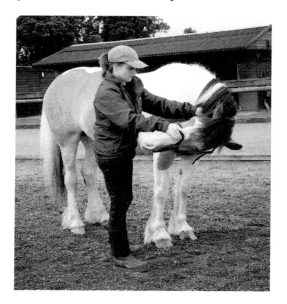

By learning to read and follow the horse's responses to your touch, equine massage and bodywork becomes a fulfilling interactive process. You are able to create a trusting bond and win the cooperation of just about any horse.

For more information about the Masterson Method® visit www. mastersonmethod.com

Shiatsu

What is Shiatsu? The direct translation is 'finger pressure'. How I describe shiatsu is as a complementary treatment that combines massage and stretching with the same principles as acupressure. The difference being that we work the whole meridian and not just pressure points although we do also use pressure points. Shiatsu is a very deep and thorough treatment that has a very profound affect on the horse.

There seems to be a bit of a misconception that Shiatsu is the 'beauty treatment' of therapies and you only do it as a treat and because its nice. This could not be further from the truth.

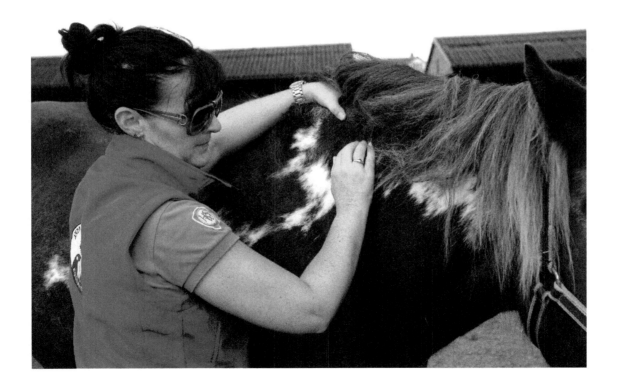

Shiatsu not only fixes physical problems but it also works on physiology and mental state, so it can treat digestive problems, circulatory issues, the immune system and the lymphatic system to name but a few .

How does this happen? By working the meridian that relates to the specific problem you are balancing the energy within and in turn creating equilibrium in the body and the system you are working.

I find it easier for people to understand by comparing the meridians to a hose pipe. If the hose pipe has a knot in it, the water does not flow, it is full at one end and empty at the other.

A Shiatsu practitioner is trained to find that knot, release the knot and allow the energy to flow and balance itself, which in turn leads to the body functioning correctly. The knot can be a physical thing where there is tension or a spasm in a muscle or it can by a physiological thing where the release of the knot allows the system to balance and function correctly.

How do we do this? Each horse is different and is treated individually, they all also react differently. I have yet to come across a horse who has not responded well to Shiatsu they all relax and get completely involved in the treatment.

Firstly we would do a body sweep of the horse and see if we could feel anything and see how the horse reacts. It is important that the horses behaviour is acknowledged throughout the treatment. There are

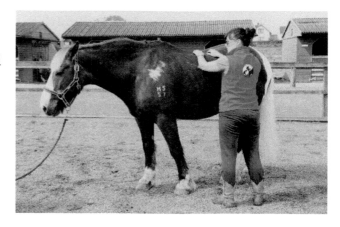

various diagnostic techniques used to ensure the horse is getting the correct treatment. One of which is working Bl meridian and feeling what is happening under the diagnosis points (I cannot go into any more detail than this here or it will get too involved) Bl meridian runs along either side of the horses spine and you will see from the picture that the horse totally relaxes as soon as this is worked.

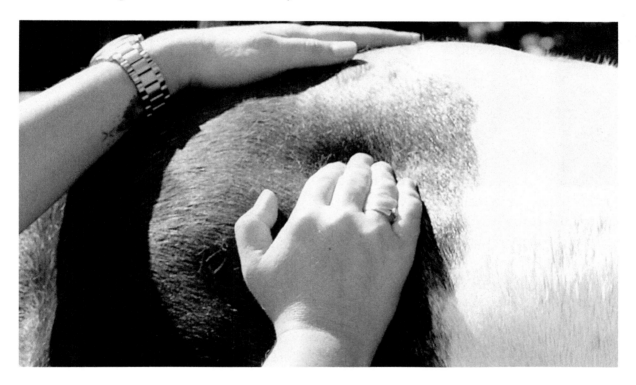

With what is felt from the horse coupled with information given by the owner, a decision is made on what is best to be worked on the horse. I am mainly driven by what I feel from the horse, as this ensures I work what the horse actually needs at that specific time.

A Shiatsu treatment treats the full horse and not just the bits we are told are an issue. This is because what we as an owner/rider, see or feel manifesting in the horses behaviour or way of going is quite often the symptom and not the cause. By treating the whole horse this means that we treat the symptom and also the cause. This in turn gives a more permanent fix.

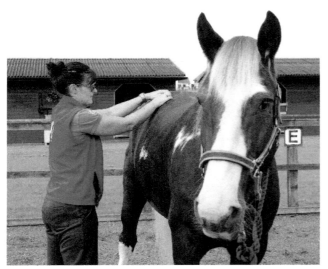

I explain Shiatsu as a bit like peeling an onion, the initial treatment takes away the first couple of layers and removes all the immediate tension and imbalances, the second treatment gets deeper and each treatment thereafter you end up having the cause of the problem exposed.

Shiatsu supports horses in many ways. A common problem and one that is easy for you to visualise is kissing spine, it will never cure the kissing spine but it

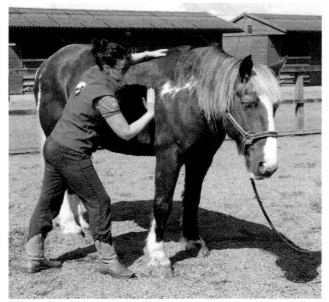

works on keeping the muscles in optimum condition therefore supporting the structure of the horse's spinal column. Also the abdomen is supported and strengthened also helping support the spine. Due to the energy side of Shiatsu, circulation is also supported and kept in balance which in turn enables muscles to stay in peak condition and in turn allow your horse to perform to the best of its ability.

A treatment works by using both energy and massage, energy by working meridians and pressure points and also works muscles by energy, and massage techniques and stretching.

Some of these are shown in the pictures you can see.

As you can also see here the horses get into a completely relaxed state which enables the muscles to be worked deeply if there is a lot of tension. It is really good for horses that get a bit worried and are nervous of deep massage because by using energy we can completely relax the muscle and remove tension and spasms without the horse objecting while staying pretty relaxed.

The treatment also gives the horses detox and they quite often take a huge drink straight after the treatment. I also have some clients who lie down and go to sleep after and or even during the treatment!

They also yawn a lot which is fantastic because it shows how relaxed they are but is also a way in which they release tension so helps their mental and emotional well-being.

Prevention is always better than cure. Everything we ask of our horse is against what nature intended so the least we can do is ensure they are kept in optimum condition.

Shiatsu will continue to work on your horse after the treatment is

finished due to the fact that the energy that has been moved/balanced will continue to do so which in turn has a knock on affect on other systems in the body.

Regular Shiatsu treatments can prolong the onset of various problems by supporting the horses' physical, mental and physiological well-being and can keep symptoms at bay which in turn helps to reduce the affect of the cause.

The horses always feel different after a treatment, they in turn ride much better. A horse who feels

good can jump higher, move more freely, stretch easier, be generally happier in themselves and all these things improve everything that we do with our horses whether they are competition horses or happy hackers and everything in between. We love our horses so it's our duty to keep them in optimum condition.

This is a very brief insight into Shiatsu because it is very difficult to explain things without getting into too much detail. For more detailed information there are various books about shiatsu available or information can be found on the TESA website.

The pictures taken are for the purpose of seeing how the horses react and not as a tutorial, some positions are slightly moved to get the best angle, light and shade for the photographs.

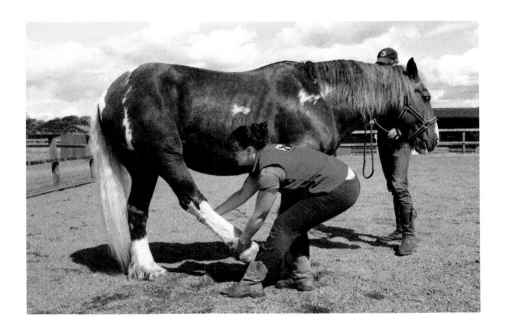

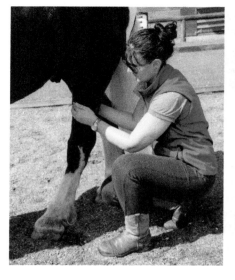
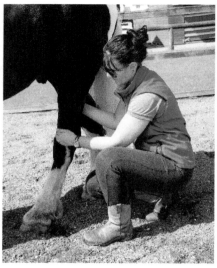

Farrier

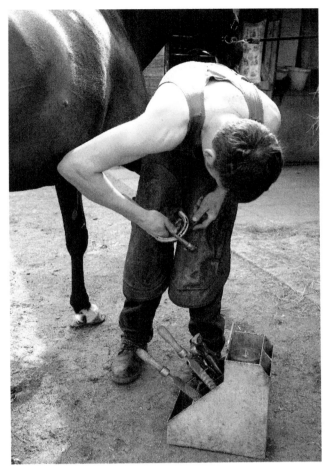

The old adage 'No foot, no horse' is very true and it is absolutely vital that you take good care of your horse's feet.

There are two main schools of thought on this matter, people who wish their horse to remain barefoot and those who are happy to have their horses shod. Feelings can run quite high on both sides and we do not wish to get into a debate about this, however suffice to say, if your horse is sound and comfortable barefoot then great but if they are lame or sore barefoot then perhaps you should consider putting on shoes. There are exceptionally good quality hoof boots (covers for horse's hooves without iron shoes) available on the market today that can be put on a barefoot horse that is working on the roads or stony ground so this might be a compromise. Basically you should do what is best for the horse. Most people do have shod horses so we will cover how a farrier would shoe a horse.

The first steps for the farrier is to remove the old shoes.

He will begin by 'knocking up the clenches'. This is the end of the nails that can be seen on the outside of the horse's hoof. He will use a small chisel like tool called a buffer and a hammer to do this.

He will slot the buffer underneath the nail end and hammer it up to 'unhook' it from the foot.

He will do this for all of the nails.

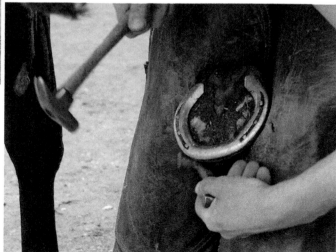

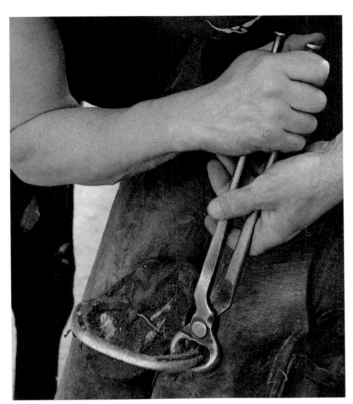

Using the pincers he will gently lever the old shoe off the foot working from heel to toe being careful not to break the horn of the foot.

Depending on how much growth there is on the foot the farrier will either use hoof cutters or a rasp to gently file away the unwanted horn.

There are two sides to the farrier's rasp, one has a coarse cut edge for use on the shoes and the other a fine cut edge for use on the hoof.

He may tidy up the trim with a drawing knife (blade with a hooked end) to cut away any diseased or infected horn.

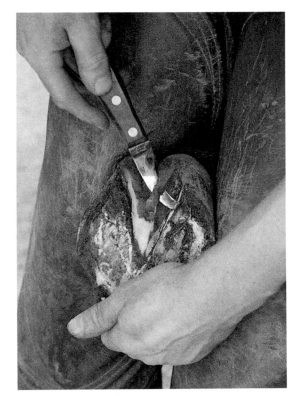

The frog of the horse also grows excess 'skin' over time and infection can get under this if not trimmed. The farrier will take care not to over trim the frog.

There are two methods of shoeing, 'hot' and 'cold'. Cold shoeing is usually only done with a young horse being shod for the first time. This means there will be no smoke from the burning horn so the horse should not get startled. It may also be seen with horses that are particularly nervous or at a show where a farrier is on hand to quickly replace a thrown shoe for competition.

Most farriers will hot shoe and to do this they must have a portable forge in their van. This is a gas oven which will raise the temperature of the iron to red/white hot making the metal malleable and easy to shape.

Some farriers will also use a sanding belt instead of the coarse side of the rasp to take the sharp edges off the shoe before fitting.

In the past a farrier would make the shoes from a single piece of iron to fit each foot individually. Nowadays this would take too much time and so they tend to have a stock of different sized shoes that should fit most horses. The farrier will select the most appropriate size and measure it against the foot of the horse.

Once satisfied that he has the best fit he will heat the shoe in the forge to red hot.

The farrier will now hammer the shoe into a shape that will fit the horse's foot perfectly.

He holds the red hot shoe in place with tongs on the anvil and using the hammer will beat the iron into shape.

Although the shoe is no longer glowing red it is still hot enough to burn to the bone so in order to take the shoe to the horse the farrier will use an instrument called a pritchel. This is also used to hammer the nail holes open on the shoe, once he has done this he will flip the shoe over and hammer the pritchel into one of the holes to carry the shoe.

Holding the still hot shoe against the horn the farrier will burn a bed into the hoof for the shoe. Because this is on the insensitive part of the foot the horse cannot feel this.

The farrier carefully checks that the shoe is sitting close to the foot. He will take the shoe off and examine the horn. If there is any part of the foot not showing heat marks it means it has not come into contact with the shoe and so the foot is not level. He may need to trim the horn again before reapplying the shoe.

Once satisfied he will put the shoe into a bucket of water to cool enough to handle.

He will then take the shoe and carefully round the edges in case the horse brushes their foot against the opposite leg when working which could cut the skin.

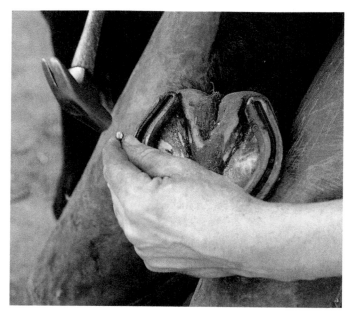

Once the shoe has cooled the farrier can nail it to the foot. He will usually start near the toe and to the inside first. The nail he is using has a slight curve or bevel in it which means as he drives it into the horn it curves outwards, avoiding the sensitive lamina.

He will use six nails (three inside, three outside) although if the horn is weak he may only use four. In the past it was traditional to have four nails on the outside and three on the inside.

He will nail as close to the toe as possible which will allow the hoof to still be able to flex at the heel and frog as the horse walks.

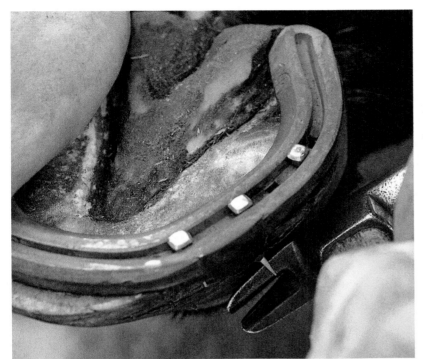

As each nail protrudes through the hoof wall he will use the hammer to 'nip' off the sharp end. He leaves a small piece still sticking out which will become the clench which he will fold down to help keep the nails in place.

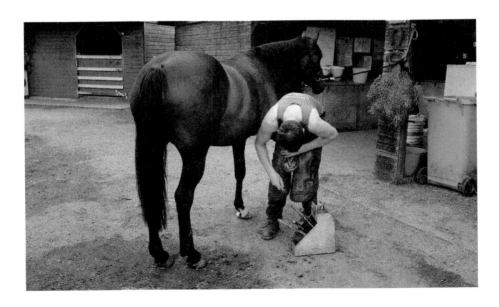

Once the shoe is nailed on he will put the foot on a stand to allow him to rasp off any horn that may be overlapping and to fold down the clenches and make sure they are flush to the hoof to prevent them catching and cutting the horse's leg.

Dental Care

It is also a vital part of your horse's well being to ensure good dental health. There are specialist equine dentists or specialist dental veterinary surgeons who can help you with ensuring your horse is comfortable in their mouths.

We use our vets to maintain dental health in our horses and in order for a thorough examination to take place they will usually place a halter with a metal gag onto the horse. This has flat plates that the horse's front incisors fit into comfortably and is levered open to a comfortable level for the horse to keep his mouth open. This allows the vet plenty of time to examine the teeth with minimum risk of being bitten. The vet will have a head torch to allow him to see right to the back of the mouth.

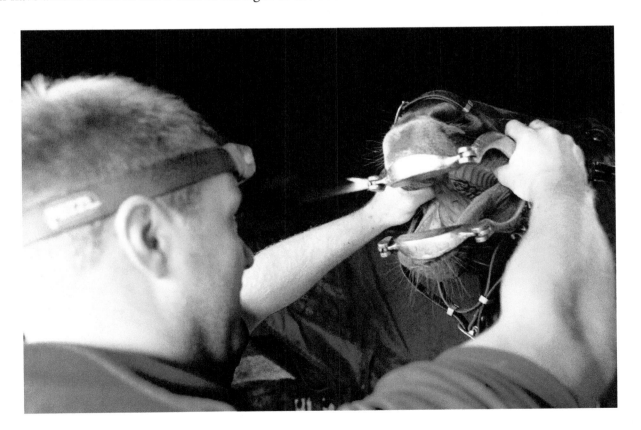

Using a specialist dental drill, the vet will gently guide the end into place in the mouth to quickly grind down any sharp edges that may have appeared.

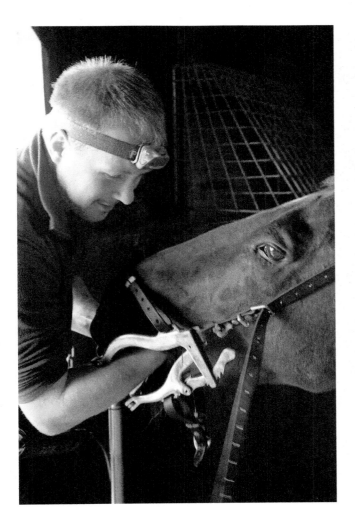
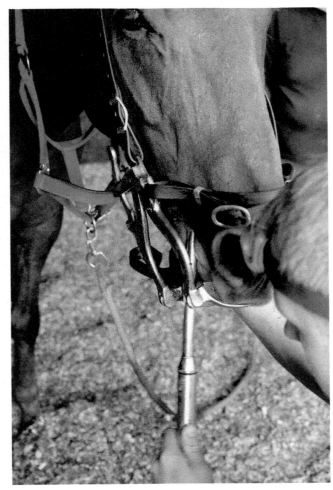

He will work on any tricky to reach parts with a finer dental rasp to ensure the horse has no sharp hooks or gaps in their teeth which can cause pain and discomfort.

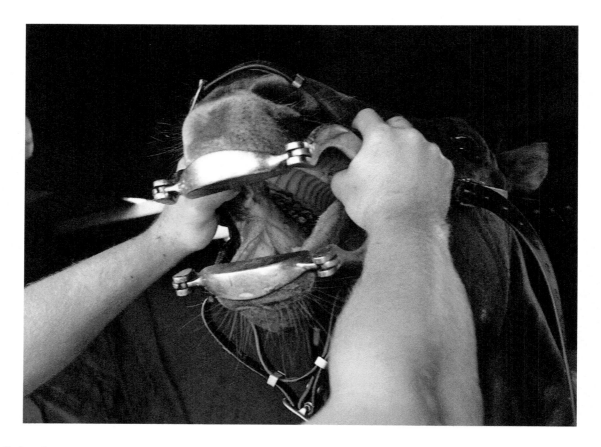

He will finish with a quick check to ensure he has not missed any potential problems.

Chapter Four - Assessing Us

"A beautiful day begins with a beautiful mindset. When you wake up, take a second to think about what a privilege it is simply to be alive and healthy. The moment you start acting like life is a blessing, I assure you it will start to feel like one."
Unknown

Where am I today. We think one of the most overlooked aspects of horsemanship is self-assessment, of where we are at that particular moment, on that particular day. There is no point in taking any baggage that you have and emptying the case in front of your horse but unfortunately that's exactly what a lot of people do. Take some time to clear your thoughts before you connect with the horse.

It's good practice every day to get into the habit of doing a quick systems check, just to see where we are at that particular time. We have to be aware of how much our energy, processing and intent can directly affect the horse. Horses are subtle animals and we tend to be at the other end of this scale, in order to work with them effectively we must have the ability to tune in to the frequency they are on in that moment. This is by no means easy but this is the fun part.

Physical fitness, are we physically fit enough to do the job? Now we're in no way saying that you need to be in the gym every day but it does help to have a basic level of fitness. Your own mental and physical well being will directly and indirectly influence your horse.

Breathing, is such an important part of how we not only deal with our fitness but it also plays a big part in how we interact with horses. Effective breathing has great value on the ground but even more in your ridden work. It allows you to blend correctly with your horse in all places and is an invaluable training aid.

As a rule we are looking to breath out on the exertion, you can try this by filling a bucket of water, pick it up while you hold your breath and repeat the exercise and exhale this time, you should see a big difference. Also with correct breathing you will get proper muscle structure especially in your core. There is a good publication on the subject of breathing, the book is by Donna Farhi and is called The Breathing Book.

Confidence, is the most fragile of human conditions. You can be the most confident person in the world and lose it over night. There is no set formula for regaining your confidence once it has been lost. It's all a mind field, and I'm using the term 'Mind Field' literally. Some people get their confidence back quickly, for some it takes a little longer, possibly with a lot of support. It happens to us all at some point in our lives and it may not be directly related to our horse work but can manifest there and in other areas of our lives.

Being confident around horses on the ground, where we are more vulnerable, allows the horse a point of reference that he can settle and let go any underlying issues or if necessary you can use your confidence to set up proper boundaries with a horse who may need more assertive guidance.

Teacher/student, almost all really great teachers are eternal students, they are always refining and refreshing their skill base and are humble enough to move from teacher to student without it bruising their egos. There are always new things to learn and fresh approaches that will add value to your own particular skill set.

One of the things we focus on, when we are teaching, is being very clear in the advice we give to our students and not using over technical jargon, what we refer to as, over indulgent techno speak. That being said we do have to be able to talk shop with our students and other professionals such as vets but as a rule we try to keep things simple and user friendly.

"There is always a way".
Mother Nature

Life skill, experience is good depending on what you have been exposed to and this is where the conflict lies. On the one hand you've spent twenty years doing things a certain way, for example, you've been exposed to a harsher way of dealing with horses, then you get a position on a yard with a more sympathetic way of dealing with horses. On the one hand your C.V. reads well, you have all the necessary skill-set to do the job but the way you go about is, shall we say, abrasive. It's up to people to educate themselves to be able to see a persons life skill/experience, most good practitioners wear it like a second skin, it looks very natural and effortless, whether their dealing with horses or people. This is a pretty big part of our tool box.

The topics above are just some of the areas that we should expect to look at with regard to self-analysis. It may look a lot but when you break things down everything blends into the other. If we look at the four stages of learning for example:

Unconscious incompetence - I didn't know I couldn't do it

Conscious incompetence - now I know I can't do it

Conscious competence - I can do it with a little thought

Unconscious competence - I do it automatically

There is a clear progression of information and how we act upon it. We are not saying that if you follow these guidelines that you will be a genius but it does allow us to find where we are and can clarify what we need to work on to get where we need to be. Another factor is how we process information, are we, kinesthetic (learn by doing), visual (learn by seeing and writing), auditory (learn by listening). The more we practice, be it physically or mentally, the more embedded it becomes in our neurology.

As you can see, the path of least resistance starts with us, we carry this to not only our horse work but all other areas of our lives. If we are always working this way then it becomes a reflex, we are available to our horse at any moment. As we have said earlier, we wear our ethos, it's like putting on an old pair of boots, they are comfortable, familiar and made for the job. Now we can have a look at our horse/horses.

Chapter Five - Assessing the Horse

Before we go down the behavioural route in training our horses we have to look at a few things first. Look at your horse's **conformation**, how's he made and will this have an affect on his performance? What age is your horse? This is a big factor on where we go with his training, although an older horse may be more developed making work easier, this would be dependent on what his work load has been and how much of his structure has been compromised through this work or possible injury. With a younger horse that may be a blank slate, we have to be aware of a few things, primarily his bone structure as he will still be growing.

One of the biggest problems in the horse world today is that a lot of horses are being started and competed too early which can lead to all manner of physical issues later on in life. Young horses may have really good potential, but what good is all that talent when you have to put your horse to sleep as a ten year-old because they are crippled? In nearly all the cases I've seen, the damage that was done to the animal happened in the initial training and competing of the horse and was not caused by the current owner.

Age is very important in how we assess the horse, is your horse too old for the job or to young and inexperienced? Leading on from this is **Pain**, is your horse sore? As stated above starting a young horse too early can have a direct correlation to your older horse being in pain and then presenting symptoms of that discomfort through behaviour.

Job of the Horse

What are you going to do with the horse? Are you a happy hacker/trail rider? Are you a show jumper, an event or western rider? The list goes on and is something we have to take into account. One of the main aspects of your job as a trainer or in training your horse, (especially if you are a trainer) is that you train the horse to the level of the skill set of the owner/rider. If you train the horse to a high level make sure your doing the same with the rider, if you don't do this it may lead to a lot of confusion for both horse and rider.

Boundaries

This is one of the most important things you can teach your horse. We see a lot of 'behavioural problems' that are in fact a break down in communication between the horse and their owners. The most common reason for these breakdowns is the human being reluctant to see that they have been ineffective in creating proper boundaries. If you are not clear, your horse may fill the gaps you have left and this can be the start of a lot of miscommunication.

If you set out your stall, so to speak, it clears up most things and then you can concentrate on moving forward. Another common cause for lack of boundaries is the horse being over humanized in their day to day handling, remember they are horses not humans.

Environment

How your horse is kept has a direct influence on their physical but more importantly mental well being. It common place in the UK for horses to be stabled, particularly in the winter, twenty-four hours a day, there are obvious reasons for this with regard to our climate. Our weather has increasingly become wetter over the last few years, we tend to get less cold frosty days and more longer periods of wet/cold, which, as a work environment, isn't pleasant for all involved. That being said, there are other options available to us that are more beneficial to equine physical health and especially to the horses state of mind.

*"**PEACE**, it doesn't mean to be in a place*
where there is no noise, trouble or hard work.
It means to be in the midst of those things
and still be calm in your heart."
Unknown

"Horses carry the soul when we ride, not just the body."
Mark Rashid

Make sure your horse always has access to water. The trough must be checked and cleaned regularly.

Contrary to popular belief, most horses do not need over rich grazing. Lush grazing such as ex-dairy pasture or new lay pasture can cause extreme health issues or even death. Horses fare better on rough pasture such as hill or sheep grazing with an old lay (a large variety of different grasses maturing at different times throughout the year).

One option is, depending on how much grazing you have available, select one of your fields preferably on a slope as your winter turn-out. Yes the field will get cut up and there is a chance of strains, pulled shoes or equine dermatitis (mud fever) but your horse is out and this is the most important thing. You can feed hay or haylage if necessary and you can get into a program of putting a barrier on your horse's legs for protection.

Another option, which we use, is to build winter turnout paddocks with feeders for hay/haylage, water and mineral blocks. You can have different sized paddocks which you can split the main herd into buddy groups. We made this decision a few years ago when the winters got wetter as a way of trying to accommodate the horse's need for being out and still having a herd even if it is slightly smaller. Our horses are out for up to ten hours a day, they get to socialize and get rid of any tension that has built up in their stables.

Something we hear quite a lot is 'Horses don't do that in the wild' well sorry to say that **MOST** horses don't live wild, they are kept in a greatly reduced area compared to their natural state and it is this change in environmental circumstance that has a direct correlation to some of the more negative behaviours we see in a domesticated herd. These behaviours are not always due to bad handling or poor management as some experts would have you believe.

Catching the Horse

One of the essentials when working with your horse is being able to catch them from the field. We talk at length about this later in Chapter Eight, in essence it is about trust between you and your horse.

In the above photograph you can see that the handler has the horse's attention, he is not holding the headcollar behind his back as there must be transparency in all of the work we do.

In this photograph the mare has lost focus on the handler and was about to leave. He simply regains her attention by raising his arms slightly while blocking the potential exit space.

In the right-hand picture in this sequence, the handler engages the horse to tip her nose towards him.

In this sequence, before the headcollar goes on, the handler makes physical contact with the horse by giving her a pat or stroke on the shoulder.

The photographs here show the handler preparing the horse for the headcollar to go on.

Firstly he slips the headpiece around the horse's neck, this allows him to flex her nose towards him. Slip the nosepiece over her muzzle and secure the headcollar.

Now that the headcollar is on and fastened we can lead the horse to the stable.

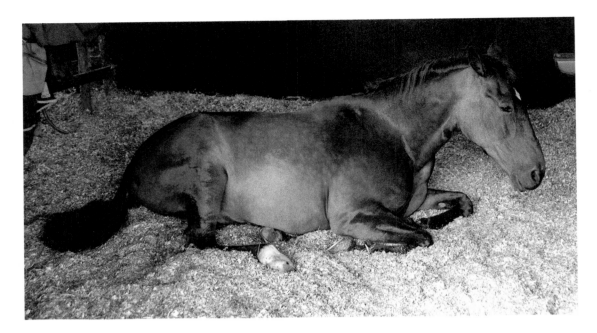

Stabling

There are countless different designs for stables be it a barn, stable block or field shelter. Most standard stables are 12ft x12ft, some are 12ft x10ft, the majority nowadays being on concrete bases with rubber matting and a sprinkle of shaving or straw to deal with urine and droppings.

We have 14ft x14ft stables and our horses are on deep litter beds. We went for this option, even though it is more costly for us, because the more room you can give your horses the better it is for them. As for the bedding, again a deep bed is more absorbent, warmer and a much better surface for horse's to rest in.

There is a partition over which the horse's can see and groom each other, again we are trying to find a compromise that is beneficial to us but more importantly the horse.

There are so many options and we could talk at length about this particular subject (environment), safe to say that we are always looking for better ways to manage our horses and improve our standards of care. If we do this, it helps us when it comes to assessing our horse's on whether or not they have any underlying behavioural issues.

In the stable, we always have to remember that horses are powerful animals and this becomes quite apparent in a stable. As with all areas in our horse work we need to be clear in our interactions, this is for safety reasons. When we are in any enclosed area with the horse we have to have clearly defined boundaries. For us this means that if we are in the stable we are in charge of that space. If you have ever been in a stable with a worried or defensive horse, you'll know that things can escalate very quickly. In an emergency you may have to get yourself or the horse out of the stable quickly but that's a moment to moment assessment.

If we are, for example, dealing with a new horse in the yard and it is apparent that he has had a limited education with regards to the appropriate boundaries around people. Firstly we would start his training in the pen or arena where there is ample room for both of us to move. Once this is established then we can take things to the stable and repeat the exercise on a smaller scale, most of this will be repetitive positioning and setting our boundaries so both horse and handler have a clearer picture. The same rules apply when grooming the horse, if they get out of position simply put them back with as little energy to get the job done. If you have to tie the horse while grooming then do so but hopefully you would only have to do this for a short period of time till the horse learns to stand still.

Grooming

Here is an example of a basic grooming kit:-

Left to right:
Mane and tail brush
Hoof pick
Dandy brush
Mane and tail conditioner
Plastic curry comb
Blade curry comb
Metal curry comb
Body brush
Grooming mit

Grooming your horse is very important for many reasons. It can keep the horse's coat in good condition, there is a therapeutic aspect for both horse and human, helps to strengthen the bond between the handler and the horse and is a fundamental part of your horse training. For example, repetitive placement, your space my space or just general boundary awareness.

Make sure when grooming the tail that you do not stand directly behind the horse. There is a blind spot in this area and even the best-behaved horse may inadvertently step back on you.

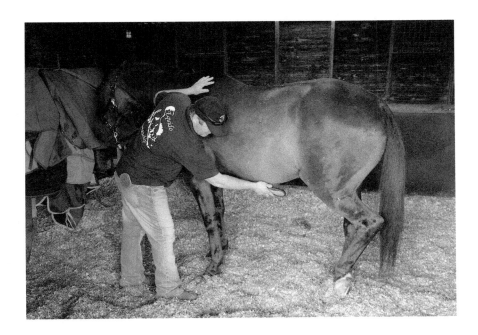

You can tell from the horse's posture in the preceding photographs that he is quite relaxed. Even though he is standing quietly, when the handler moves to brush the horse's legs, he always makes sure he maintains contact with the horse.

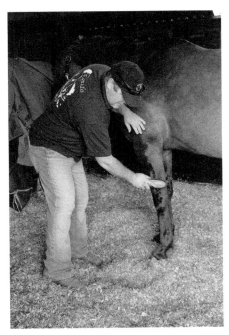

Picking Up The Horse's Feet

Most people's issues with their horse's feet usually happens when the horse is young. Some people are just too quick, too abrupt or snatch the foot up way too high, this can lead to the horse being unbalanced and worried.

Initially the young horse will try to kneel down on the foot you have lifted, especially if you hold it too high. When we work with any horse with a foot handling issue we just want to lift the foot a little while we try to work on the order that particular horse likes to lift its feet. It may be near side pairs or off side pairs or front then back pairs or they may be more comfortable working with diagonal pairs. Each horse is different and you may have to take a bit of time finding out what your horse is comfortable with. Another good tip is visualize the horse lifting the foot and give the horse a little prompt, for example, if you wanted to pick up the front near side you would start on the neck working your way over their shoulder down the forearm and hopefully by the time you get to the foot the horse is shifting their weight to allow you to lift that foot. You can use a soft rope to pick up the feet of a horse that may move or flick a kick, this allows you to keep out of the way of any danger. The rule of thumb with this method is that you only drop the foot when the leg is relaxed, once you have done this you can go back to using your hands and see how things progress from there.

There are horses however, who strike out with front or back feet, there can be countless reasons for this, pain, learned behaviour or they are defending themselves. These types of horses have to be managed

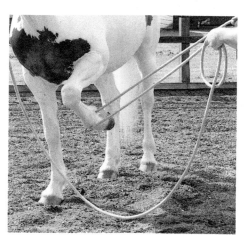

differently. We have to think of ourselves, staff, clients, farrier and the vet whose safety is paramount. If a horse was striking out so badly that it would be unsafe to put your hand in that area then we may want to use something safer like a false hand. We use a padded glove on a stick to reach in and get the horse used to things touching their legs. We also use a litter picker so there is some articulation that mimics the movement of our hand. Usually this is done after we have done quite a bit of groundwork to get the horse on board with our way of thinking. There are however some horses that are so traumatized that they may need sedated by a vet and even then they can fight the sedation. At this point the horse's owner usually has to do some soul searching.

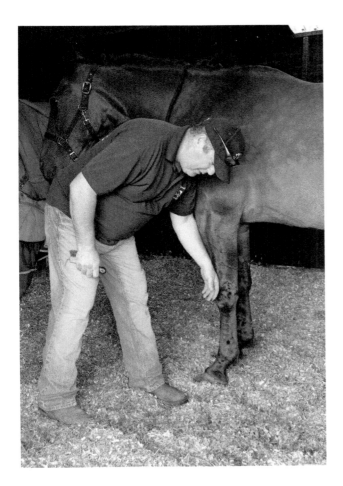 

As mentioned previously, keep a contact with the horse as you start running your hand down the leg (starting at the shoulder). This allows you to feel if the horse starts to shift their weight either to pick the leg up or to leave.

"There is always a way".
Unknown

Once you have the horse's hoof in place, always remember to work from heel to toe.

Once the foot has been picked out you can use a brush to clean the hoof and check for any damage to the sole or frog.

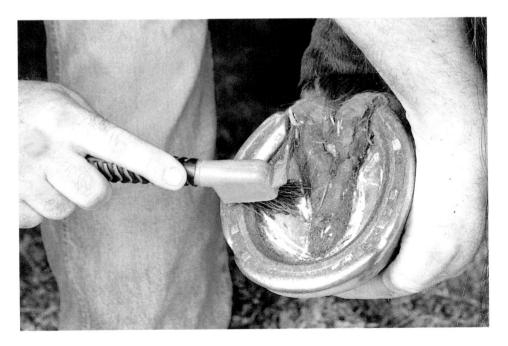

Small Changes

After taking everything we have covered above into account we are finally ready to start our work with the horse. However, before we leap in all guns blazing, there is something we must always take into consideration. Over the years we have found that, especially in the early stages, if we break down the work we are looking for from the horse into manageable learning sessions, it allows the horse time to process what they have learned.

This seems to fit in really well with most of the horses we have worked with. Some horses you have to take the small units and break them down further, other horses can manage bigger portions of information without losing the value of the work, but as a rule we usually start small and join the pieces together.

"No matter the situation never let your emotions overpower your intelligence."
Unknown

Issues

If you come across any issues during your assessment then you have to look at how deeply set the behaviour is and how you would approach rectifying it. So if we look at how we mentally process, i.e. with a phobic response, (this is a reaction to a certain stimulus that can create a negative response in us) and analyse how it affects us, then we can begin to understand how to help the horse.

The following steps are just one way to write this process, as there are many different variables:
So if we say the human process is - Fear, anger, change, acceptance, commitment, progression

And now the horse - Fear, instinct, change, acceptance, progression

Should there be a potential issue with the horse, by understanding our own fears and concerns, we can find a way forward that is more beneficial and sympathetic for both parties.

Chapter Six - Toolbox

The best tool you have when working with horses is yourself. Most people forget to use themselves properly; our bodies have a lot of meaning to the horse if used correctly. If we work on our awareness we can lessen any unwanted behaviour that the horse may present. Also with proper timing we can affect appropriate responses in the horse which can help them process their way through any underlying issues there may be.

We see so many people trying to use gadgets to get the horse going well and all they tend to do is get the horse braced and confused. The use of body work (massage) before, during and after training will hopefully benefit the horse physically and allow us to formulate a proper course of action that will fit the horse's particular physical and mental ability.

Keep Things Simple

There are so many gadgets on the market to help you train your horse, it can get pretty confusing. We use either a web halter or a rope one with various lengths of ropes or lines depending on the type of training we're working on. There are so many things we can work on using ourselves, our intellect, a halter and rope.

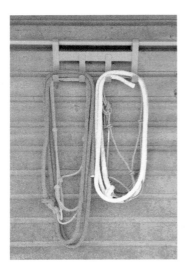  

In the pictures above, left to right, you will see two rope halters, equipment for long lining and basic bridles.

In this picture we can see a standard general purpose saddle that is more biased towards jumping (forward cut knee rolls). This is a treed saddle (has a rigid frame around which the leather is attached).

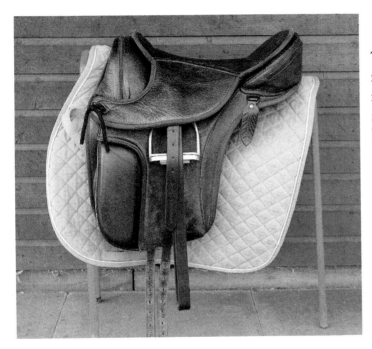

To the left is a treeless saddle (there is no rigid frame except for the front arch) which is biased for dressage (there is no forward cut knee rolls, instead they are straight). We use this saddle for backing horses as it is light and flexible.

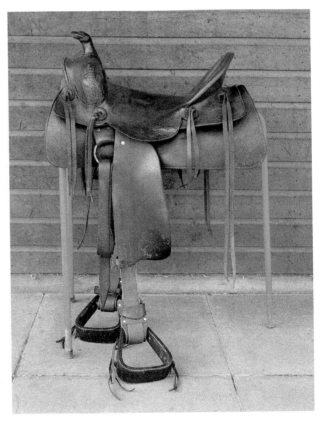

This shows a treed western saddle. This saddle is designed for general stock work, not for roping as can be seen by the single girth with a Y connector which draws down both the back and front of the saddle as the cinch is tightened.

The simplicity of the western saddle was that almost 99% of it was easily repaired by the rider if they were on the range working cattle. The ties you see are not decorative but actually lace the leather from the bottom panels up to the top panels and help hold the saddle together. They are also useful for tying equipment to.

This particular saddle is approximately 130yrs old; they were built to last.

The bridle on the left has small tassels on the brow band to help keep flies off the horse's face.

The chinks (shorter version of chaps) had fringing that would draw any moisture away from the centre where it would be evaporated as the fringes moved in the wind or would simply drop off the end of them. This helped to keep the legs of the rider as dry as possible.

In an emergency the fringes could also be cut and used to repair equipment if necessary.

Groundwork

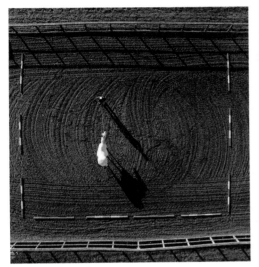

Orientation, a big part of any relationship with your horse is how you both see each other, the environment around us and how we react to it. In an ideal world we would be our horse's point of orientation, no matter where we are there is something familiar as a place of reference. This does not happen overnight, we have to earn this, in the same way the horse has to give over everything to us we have a BIG responsibility, never compromise that trust. If we can work on the horse's orientation and trust then there will always be a strong line of communication in case we come across an unfamiliar situation.

Groundwork and it's application to ridden work. There are a couple of schools of thought on this subject. On the one hand there are those who feel there is no correlation between groundwork and ridden work. And there are those people who say it has a direct bearing on how the horse performs under saddle. What I have noticed is usually both sides of the debate use groundwork, I find it odd that the people who say there is no direct link between riding and groundwork still use it as part of their horses training. There was a study done in Germany where two groups of horses were trained, one group given groundwork and the other none. What the study showed was that the horse's given groundwork were a lot calmer under saddle than the group that had no groundwork. To me this is enough of a reason to train your horse in groundwork, if it has a calming effect then that is enough of a reason to spend some time on it.

Which leads me to my next point, always be safe, we want to do the best for the horse but you can't do that if your dead or seriously injured, '**your safety outweighs the horse's safety**'.

Our good friend Mark Rashid has a nice little saying, '**you have the right to defend your position**', now before you break out the gun cabinet let me explain. There is an area, for me personally about an arms length around me, which, especially with a troubled or unfamiliar horse, is my **safety zone** I can make it larger or smaller given the particular horses needs at that moment in time but all the while trying not to compromise my safety as well.

Check Your Equipment

This is self-explanatory. Like we do with the horse and ourselves, always give your tools a quick look over for any issues like wear and damage. Repairs will usually cost less if done when you spot the damage but importantly you risk injury to you and your horse by having equipment that is not in tip-top condition.

Do Less

One of the most common faults we see people make is getting the horse to a good place then being a bit impatient and asking for more and it usually ends up in a mess. We've seen people doing a one-hour

schooling session, get it good for the first half then waste it all in the next thirty minutes because they wanted to work for the full hour. As we have discussed, get what you're looking for in small units then add them together to make it whole.

Fit it to the Horse

Whatever you are doing try to fit it to the horse in front of you. There is no point in training a horse past its own physical and mental ability, in fact it can have a real negative effect on the horse and in most cases it will take you twice as long to get to where you want the horse to be.

Techniques aren't Everything

What we mean by this is don't get too wrapped up in the technical side of things especially with a young horse. Now we're not saying be sloppy but be careful that you aren't pushing the horse away from you by being too precise. This leads us to our next heading

Don't Lose the Horse

It is so easy to push the horse into survival mode just by approaching them with the wrong feel/energy. We always want to fit in and find out where the horse is, then we adapt to what they are offering and mould it into something that is beneficial to both parties.

Availability

Are our horses available to work with us? For our part we can work on our availability all the time, so that when we go to the horse we are open, if we are available the horse will, hopefully, mirror our behaviour. Being open allows the horse a place to go. The more we are available the more we can teach the horse to look for that space, whether it is mental or physical.

Line Work

Single line work is an invaluable training tool which, if used properly, can give your horse a good start. If a youngster or if older it is good for clearing up any miscommunication with the handler. Where do we begin? Well we always give the horse a line and boundary assessment which consists of working on positioning the horse in a place which in some cases takes the pressure off of them. In other cases working the horse this way allows the horse to get out of position and be guided back in a manner that is sympathetic to the individual animal which in turn lets them know where their boundaries are. Getting your horse familiar to coming off pressure, if you teach them properly you will work with the least amount rather than the most. A lot of the work we do with the horse is directing them or taking their mind away from what they are focusing on and asking them to re-direct their focus to us or the task at hand. Work the angles.

Leading Away

The three pictures in this sequence show the starting position of leading the horse away. The picture above shows the handler standing back and away from the horse. This will help the horse have a clear line of sight of the handler's intention.

In these pictures the handler walks directly down the horse's flank, on reaching the hindquarters the horse's nose will start to tip towards the handler which will send the quarters in the opposite direction as can be seen in the following two pictures.

Once the initial turn has finished, the horse will drop into a position directly behind the handler. From this point onwards the horse will follow the handler's footsteps. If they were to veer to the inside or the outside the handler will re-direct them back into position behind them.

The top picture shows the handler turning and preparing the horse for the halt, which is executed in the next picture. This indicates to the horse that the exercise has ended. The next sequence of photographs shows the same manoeuvre as seen from above.

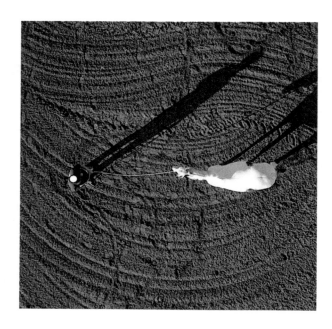
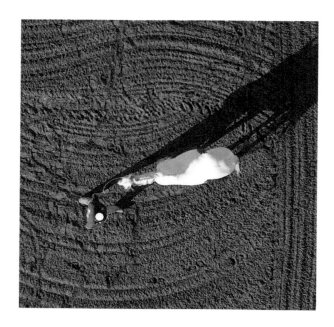

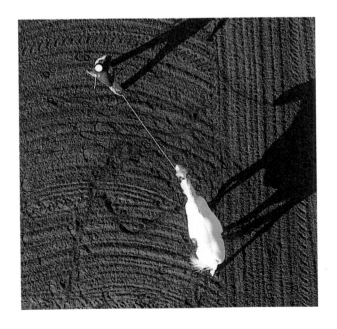
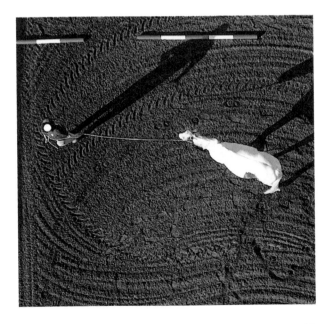

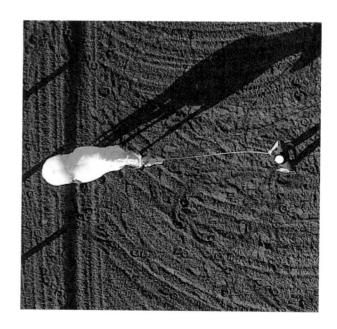

Sending Away

As before, the handler starts at a distance from the horse. We then move to the side of the horse, which opens up one side more than the other, this gives the horse a clear indication of where you are going.

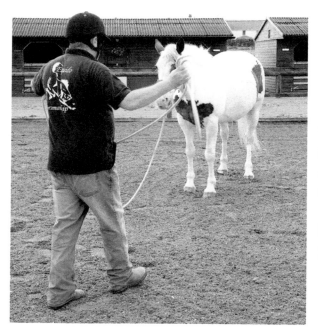

We move in towards the horse's shoulder whilst indicating to the horse, with our posture, the direction they should follow. This sequence can be clearly seen in the picture opposite and below.

In the following pictures you can see how this movement progresses and how the horse yields to the handler's left.

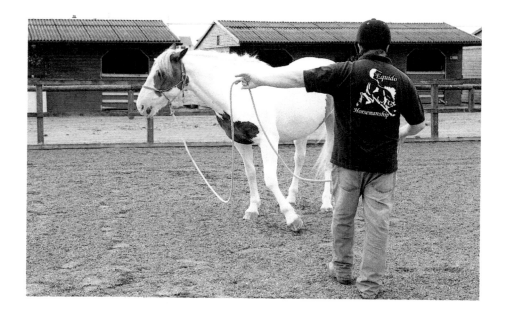

The handler is now in what is known as the drive position, which is slightly behind the girth line of the horse. This enables the handler to direct the horse forwards.

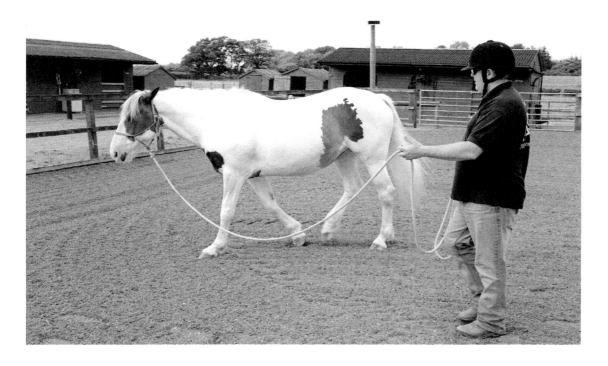

The handler moves the rope coil into their left hand. The right hand slides to the midway point in the line and tips the horse's nose towards him.

This prompts the horse to swing the hindquarters away, turning their head to face the handler. This indicates to the horse that the exercise had ended. The next sequence of shots shows the same exercise viewed from above.

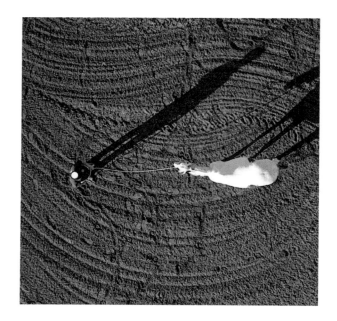

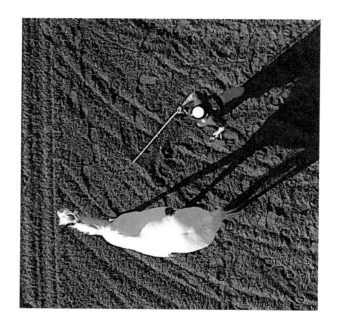

"Empty your mind, be formless, shapeless, like water"
Bruce Lee

We can also use the line work to get the horse familiar with things like how to pick up their feet and prep work for backing/saddling the horse. You can use line work for leading the horse up to the mounting block in a manner that won't stress them. If you do this correctly you'll be able to get on them from anywhere and you will find that the training will last a lifetime. Groundwork can also be used as the prep work for loading, getting your horse ready for lateral flexion would be done on the line, as well as getting in time with your horse's foot falls. There are so many ways to get your horse with you by just working them in a line and halter. One of the things we try to do when working through the horses paces is to think the beat you're looking for before you initiate it so gradually, through training, the horse picks up more of your feel/energy.

Straightness is another aspect we would work on. If we prepare the horse on the ground to look for the centre then it will find this same point between the reins in the ridden work. There are a lot of simple exercises that you can do on the line that will plant a seed for when you start riding.

Following the Feel

In the next sequence of photographs we are developing the horse's ability to give to the slightest contact. At the same time we are exposing them to more aspects of line work.

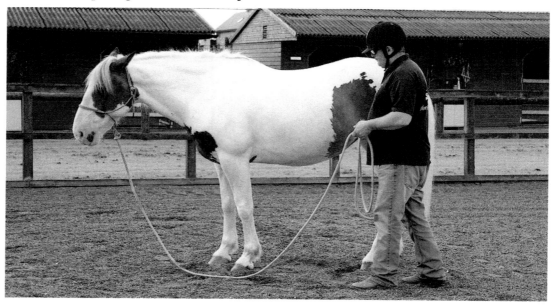

In this section we are working on the horse's contact with us. These simple exercises help to iron out most issues that the horse may have with lines and their ability to follow direction from the handler.

Here we are preparing to ask the horse to release away from us.

Facing forwards, in the same direction as the horse, we gradually walk backwards and step across behind the horse's hindquarters. NOTE: the horse that we are working with in these photographs is very comfortable with someone behind them.

It is good practice to work with a horse that you know is safe so that you can become more familiar with the exercise.

In the above photographs we are on the other side of the horse and we now gradually pick up the slack in the line. What we must be very careful not to do is to pull the horse around; instead we should allow the horse time to 'think' their way around with the lightest of contacts.

As you can see above the line is slack and holds no tension, this allows the horse to think her way through the exercise.

Once the horse turns towards the handler we can continue with our leading exercise in a circular motion.

The picture above shows that the horse has become slightly confused about her next step.

In the bottom picture you can see the handler redirecting her and helping her towards a positive outcome.

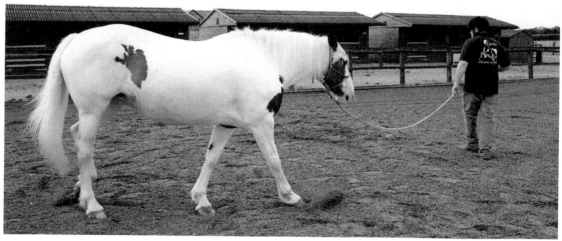

These two pictures show a continuation of the leading work where the horse leads in behind the handler.

In these photographs you will see a variation of the previous exercise. Instead of walking behind the horse initially, we pass the rope up and over the horse's withers.

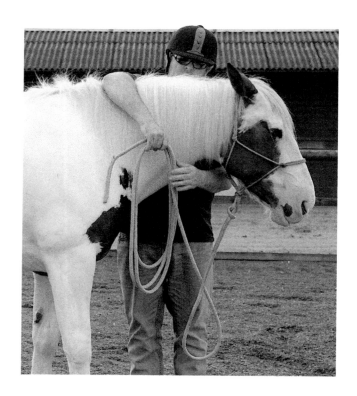

*"What you think about activates
a vibration within you."*
Abraham Hicks

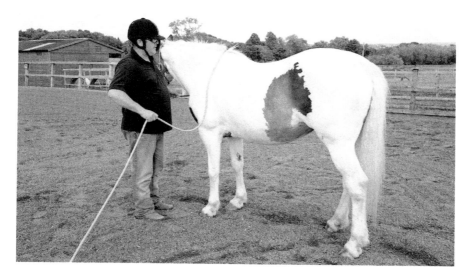

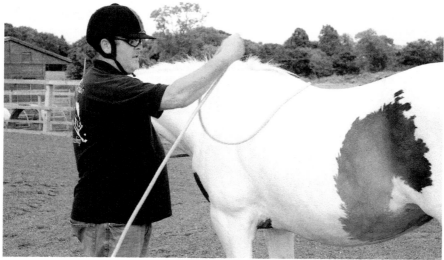

Now that we have the line over the withers we can walk the line gradually down the horse's back until the line is sitting around the quarters. Be aware that you should keep your free hand just below the halter on the line or on the knot, this will allow you to help the horse stay in position. This is an ideal technique for horses that are a bit sensitive to the line and keep the handler in a safe position.

*"It is the supreme art of a teacher to awaken joy in
creative expression and knowledge"*
Albert Einstein

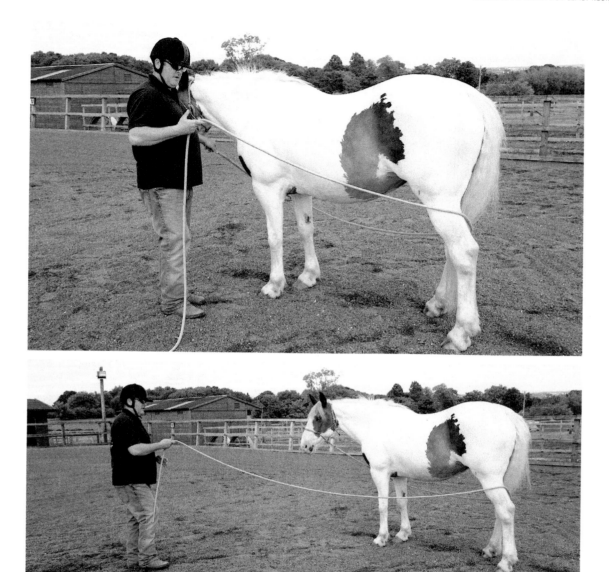

As you can see from the pictures above the handler is in a safe area and allows him to continue with the exercise as previously outlined.

Again in the photographs above you can clearly see where we make contact.

In the next sequence of four photographs we can see the completion of the exercise.

Always reward your horse and finish on a positive note.

Prep Work for Girthing

Girthing can sometimes be an issue for horses, especially those with sensitive skin or who have been started insensitively. Usually when doing our line work, in preparation for girthing, we will use the line around the horses barrel to assess where the horse is mentally and physically.

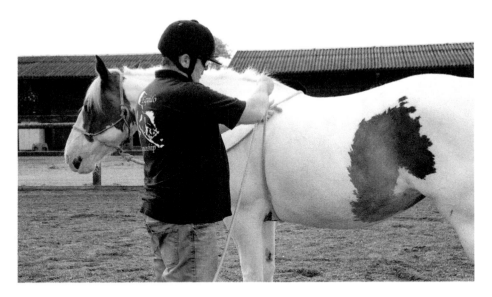

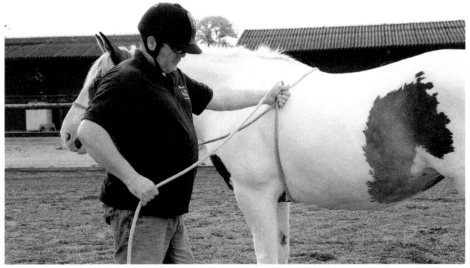

As you can see in the pictures above we have put the line around the horse's girth area and slowly apply pressure. If the horse is happy and standing quiet we will release the contact then re-apply, increasing the tension progressively. You can see this in the following sequence.

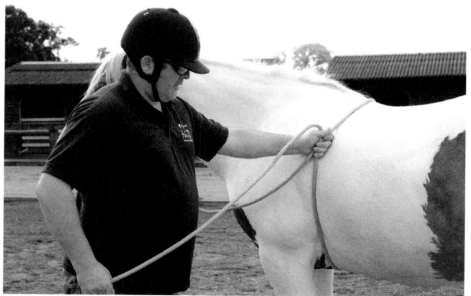

Walking with the Girth Line

Another exercise that we include in our line work is walking the horse with the girth line around her. The next series of photographs briefly shows how you can use the line to apply contact on and off in not only the girth area but also other parts of the horse's body.

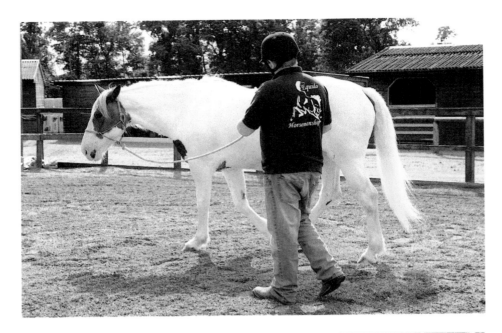

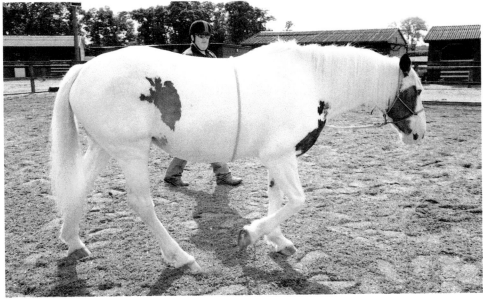

As always finish your work on a good note.

Backing Up

There are some schools of thought that feel that teaching your horse to back up leads to napping, especially when ridden. However, we strongly disagree. If you have ever watched horses playing in a field with each other they in fact back up naturally. When we train the horses in groundwork, we feel that to have balance, the horse needs to know how to move in all directions. This is something that is also carried forward into ridden training.

As in previous exercises we start at distance so that the horse has plenty of time to work out what we are looking for.

When the horse backs up they should move backward in diagonal pairs. In the photographs above the horse has misinterpreted what the handler is looking for and is thinking about stepping to the outside.

Here the handler has redirected the horse back to the original task and kept the horse settled and relaxed.

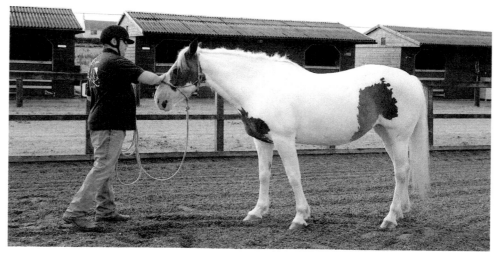

As you can see by the horse's expression in the final photograph there was no stress involved whilst doing the exercise.

NOTE: When backing the horse up, if the horse is relaxed and only gives you one step then take that. Build up gradually to a sequence of steps.

Lifting the Legs/Preparing for Farrier

NOTE: Horses by nature are aware of their legs as this is their primary method of transport and defence. **It is not your farrier's responsibility for training your horse to pick up his/her feet. That responsibility lies with the owner.**

If your farrier or vet needs to look at your horse's feet it is important that your horse is familiar with contact in this sensitive area. In the next series of pictures we are demonstrating how you can pick up the horse's leg safely using a rope. The key point in doing this is that the leg is picked up and placed back down in a relaxed state.

Mounting Block Work

The following sequence of photographs shows how we would prepare a horse to be comfortable around the mounting block. Horse's can be suspicious of anything above their heads. Again, as in previous exercises, we start with the horse at distance and walk them in one step at a time until they reach the mounting block.

Once the horse is close to the handler then they can reassure the horse by patting and rubbing the horse's head and neck. If done correctly the horse will have a positive outlook when approaching the mounting block.

NOTE: The poles at the rear of the mounting block are only there to guide the horse.

Keeping the horse in a relaxed state of mind, the handler moves away from the mounting block giving the horse a time out before continuing with the exercise.

Now the handler is back at the mounting block we can see in the next sequence of photographs from a different viewpoint.

Now the horse is comfortable at the mounting block we can start adding other aspects. In the pictures above the handler is leaning across the horse and touching the offside ribcage this also allows the horse to see the handler in his right eye, this helps when we begin to back the horse to saddle.

In the previous pictures and above, we are beginning to get the horse accustomed to pressure on both sides, again this is good preparation for backing.

The following photographs show the same pattern as seen from above.

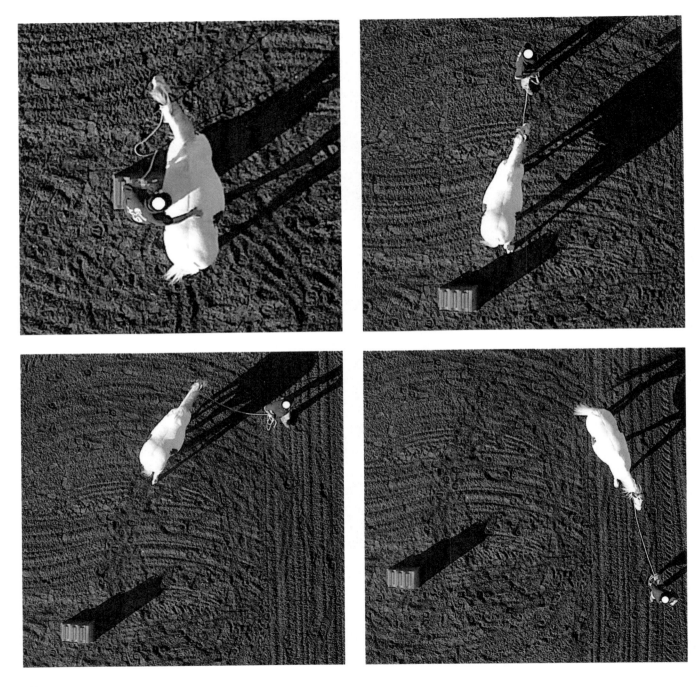

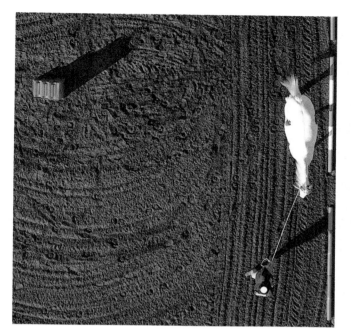
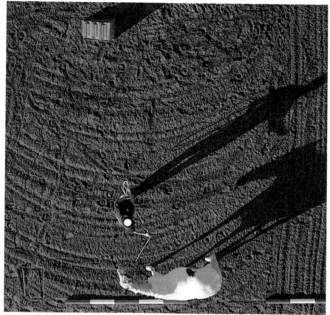
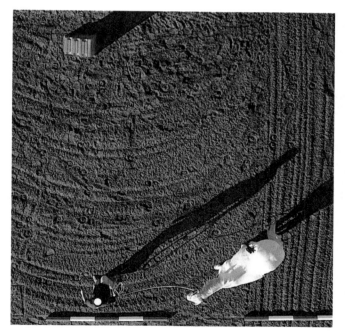

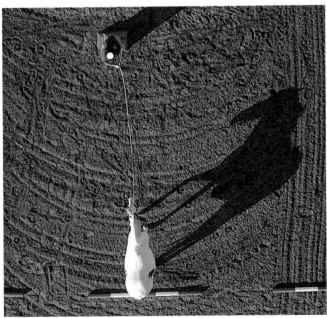

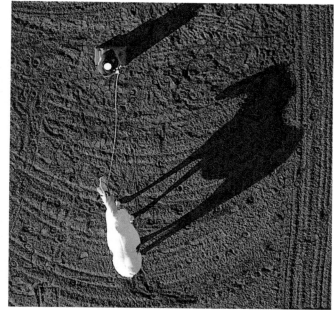

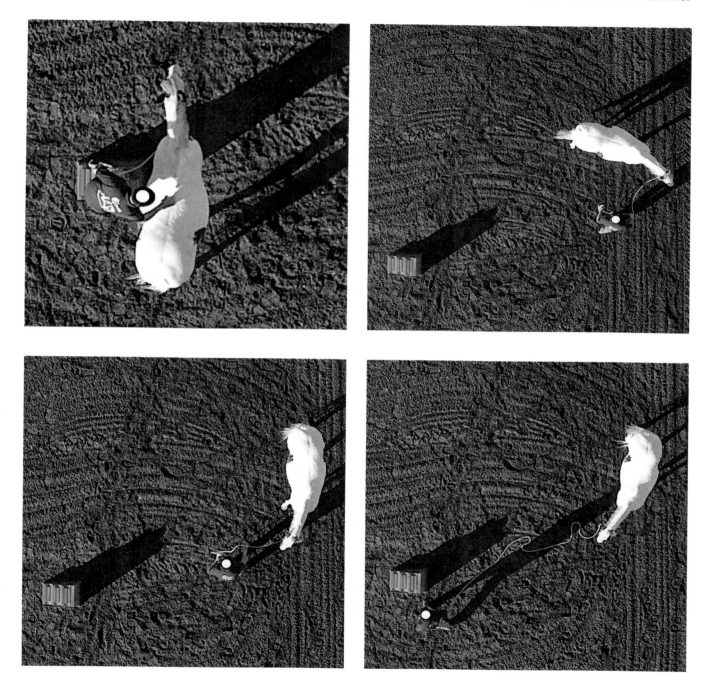

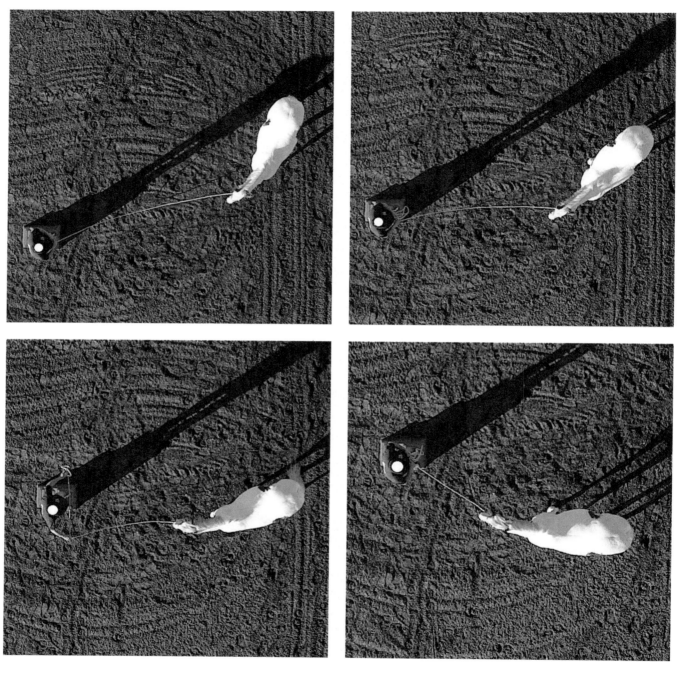

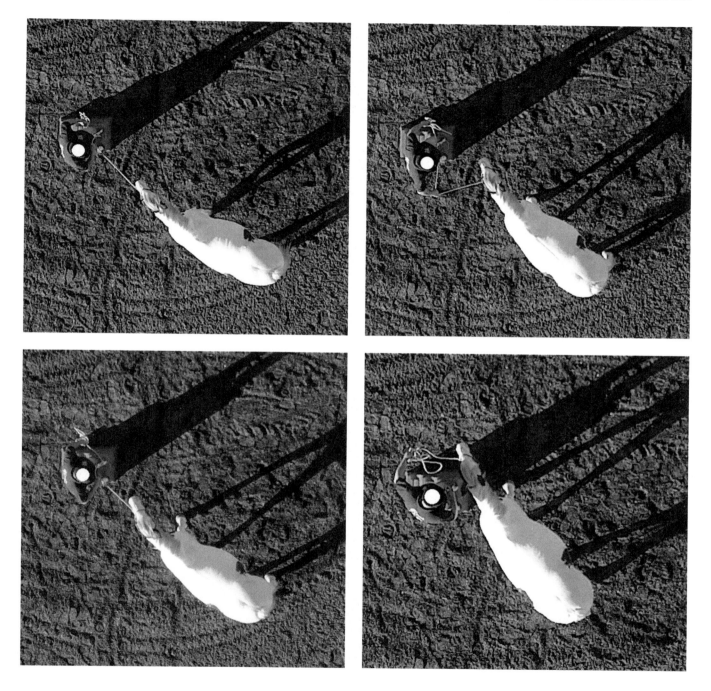

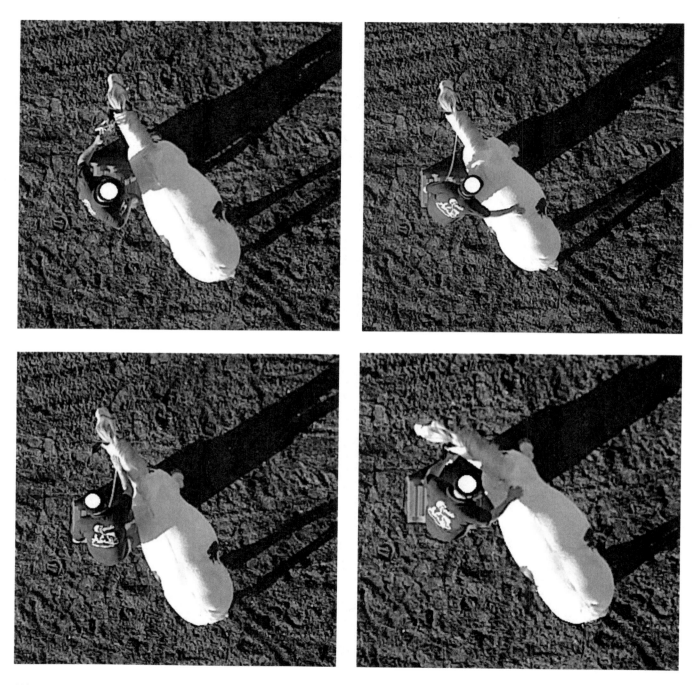

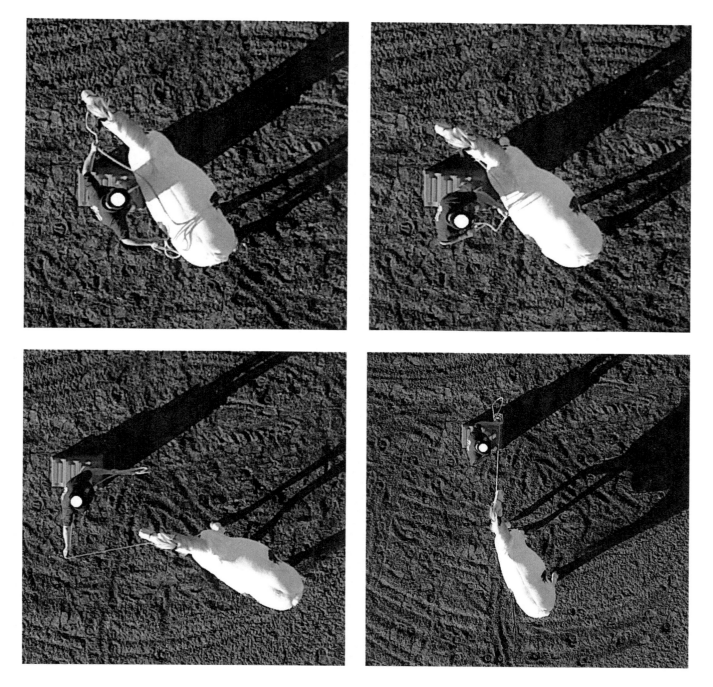

Preparing for Saddle

Backing a horse or re-backing a horse is, if done correctly, a skill or even an art form. What tends to happen, generally, when people back their horse is that things are done all too quickly. Usually a big factor in any problems that arise is the horse not being mentally or physically sound or mature enough. There is a lot of pressure put on, not only horses, but also their owners to get their horses moving on in their education. It takes focus not to be drawn into pushing, not only your horse, but yourself into doing too much with your horse over a short period of time. If you take your time and let the horse mature whilst doing some really good prep work you should have very little trouble when it comes to the riding side of things.

When you speed up any process chances are things won't work out the way you thought. We live in a society that is ruled by the clock which unfortunately doesn't suit any horse or any animal for that matter. We are constantly seeing horses with physical problems that are a direct result of being worked too hard at an early age. The same applies to horses that are mentally scarred because too much pressure has been

placed upon them far too early. In our opinion, these practices need to be reviewed. Your horses will be around far longer (failing accident or injury) doing the job you choose for the simple fact that you took your time educating them and waited until they were physically and mentally capable of doing what was asked of them.

All of the previous work we have done with the horse and lines will have built a bond of trust with the handler.

Because in the UK the climate is quite wet, most horses are familiar with rugs being put on them and they are also familiar with straps crossing beneath their belly. This can be beneficial with the backing process because they are already comfortable with things being put on and taken off.

Even so, before we put the saddle on we would use a saddle cloth to find out the horse's state of mind.

As you can see in these photographs we are using a saddle cloth to prepare the horse for the saddle.

NOTE: The horse we are using has been backed so is already comfortable with this, she is being used for demonstration purposes only. Your horse should be in the same calm state that she is demonstrating before continuing with the exercise.

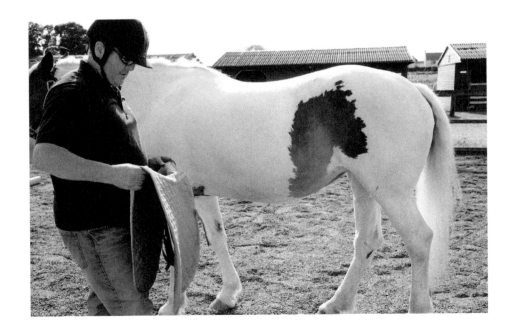

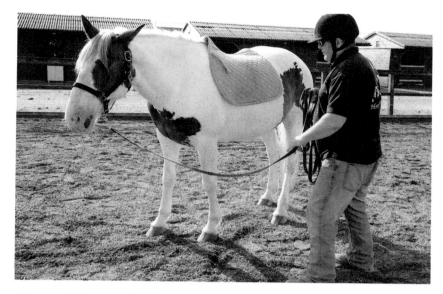

In the picture above the handler has organised the long line so that in an emergency the whole line can be let out. By doing this the handler still has a free hand if they need to take the saddle off should the horse show any signs of stress.

Initially the handler familiarises the horse with the saddle. As you can see there is no girth, no saddle cloth or stirrups attached. This allows the horse to get used to the basic weight of the saddle sitting on her back. The saddle being used is a lightweight treeless saddle.

The handler removes the saddle in the same way that the saddle pad was removed over the horse's quarters.

Having repeated the previous exercise a few more times, the handler now attaches the girth.

Be aware that you may have to adjust the girth a few times which allows the horse even longer to get familiar with you working around the tack.

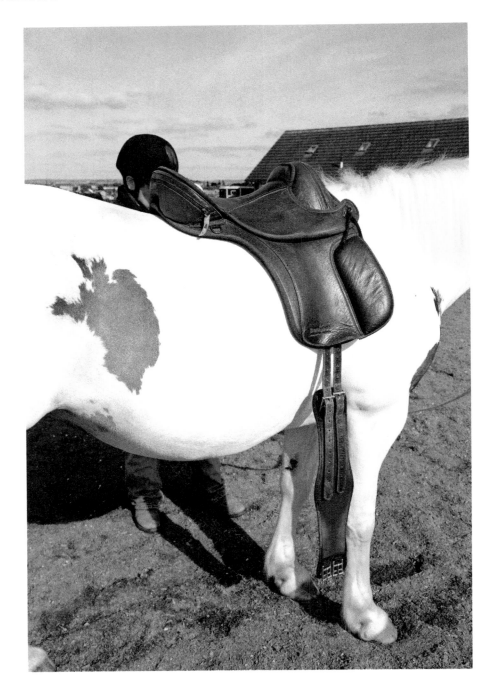

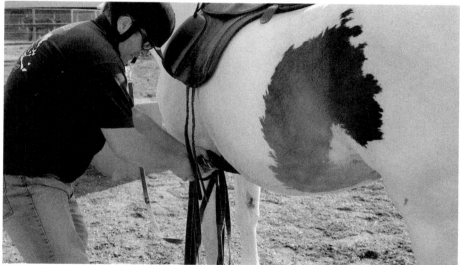

Now the handler places the girth into position for the girth straps to be fed through the buckles. Again this would be repeated a few more times to allow the horse to become comfortable with the process. Once satisfied then you can move on to the next stage.

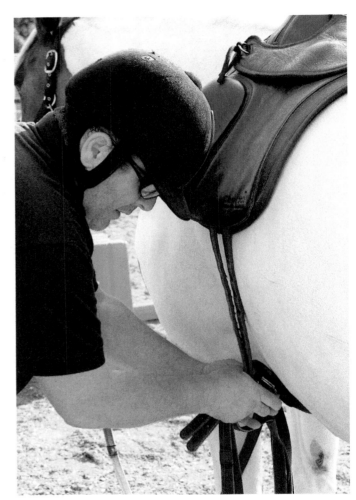

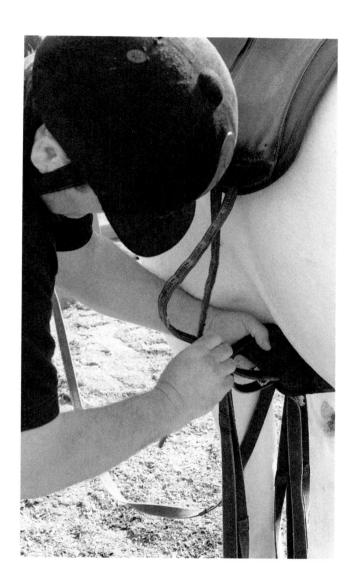

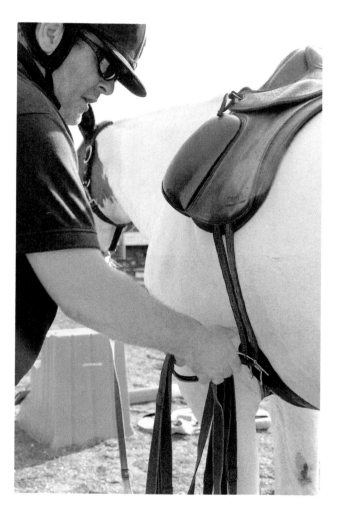

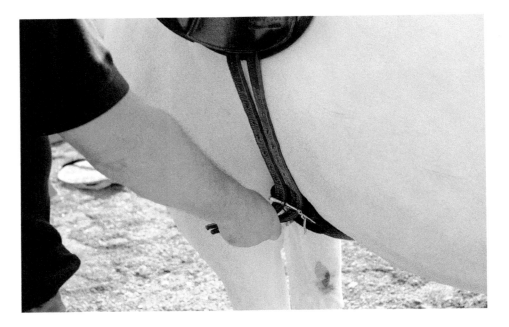

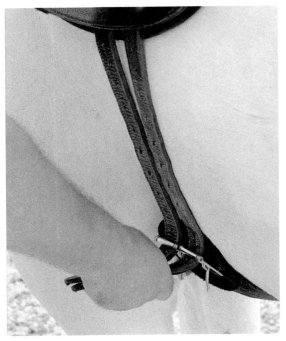

In the next sequence of photographs you will notice that the pins of the buckles have not been secured to allow the handler to tighten and loosen the girth gauging the horse's response.

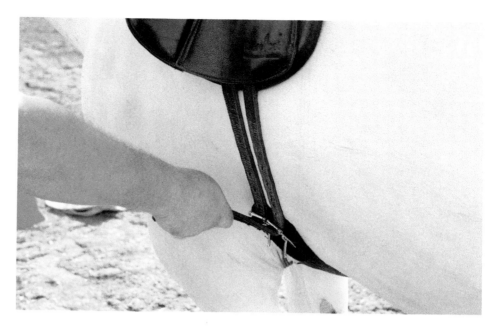

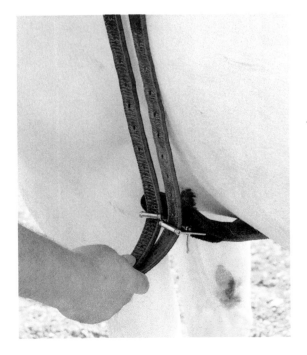

"The horse is a great equaliser, he doesn't care how good looking you are, or how rich you are, or how powerful you are. He takes you for how you make him feel."
Buck Brannaman

One final step the handler could do before securing the girth is asking the horse to move whilst they are holding the girth straps.

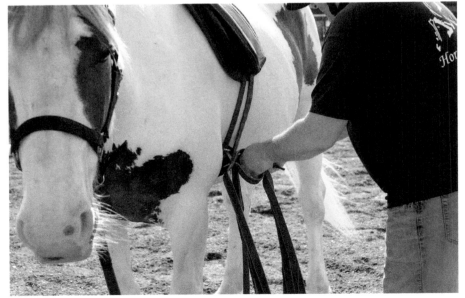

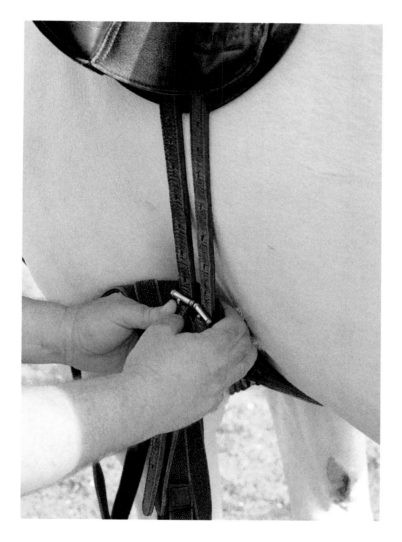

In this photograph you can see the handler finally securing the girth whilst making sure that it is just tight enough to keep the saddle in place.

NOTE: The girth straps on either side have been left loose, this has been done on purpose allowing the horse's front legs to be brushed by them. This prepares them for the eventuality of their foreleg touching the riders boot.

Here the handler is attaching the stirrups. This allows the horse to stand with the girth tight and become accustomed to other parts of the saddle.

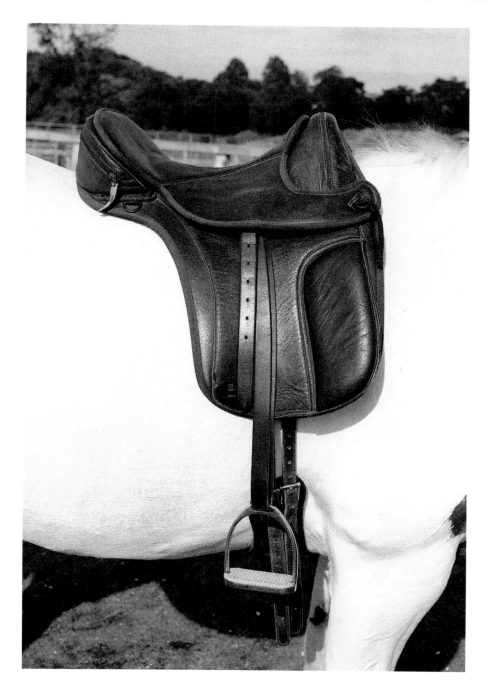

The horse is now standing with the full saddle and saddle cloth.

NOTE: With horses that are more nervous it may be advisable to have a breast girth attached to prevent the saddle slipping back.

"Fear is not your enemy.
It is a compass point in you to an area where you need to grow."
Steve Pavina

Bitting

After you have done a good job backing your horse we come to bitting or not bitting, that is the question. We see a whole bunch of 'natural horse people' who have the horse barefoot, bitless and bareback because that is natural for the horse and that's cool. Others do combinations of equipment and that is also, cool. But the fact is **nothing** we do with horses is natural, now we have that out of the way, let's look at how we can help the horse and give them the individual direction needed.

There are reasons to bit a horse and some reasons not to but we should try to avoid blindly following one way over the other. What we should be focusing on is finding a method of directing the horse that is sympathetic to them and also the rider. **Any piece of equipment is only as effective as the hand that directs it,** this is one of our mantras. We have seen people ride bitless with no feel, sawing on the horse's head with a rope halter, likewise we have witnessed people move from snaffle to pelham (a more severe bit) with the same lack of touch that got them into their predicament in the first place. If we talk about bits the benchmark is that the more effective the bit the better educated the hand in charge of it. Other things to take into account are your horse's mouth confirmation, depending on your findings they should direct you in what setup you can use with that horse. There are vast arrays of bits on the market, we prefer a simple snaffle, for you to choose the right one for your horse and for those who want to go bitless the choices are getting greater every year.

The point we're trying to make is, look at the bigger picture and evaluate what your options are before you get stuck doing something that sits well with you but isn't really beneficial to your horse. Usually if we back a horse we bit it separately. We may bit the horse during the groundwork sessions or we may get the backing to saddle out of the way first but we tend not to do both at once. Our feelings on this are, try not to give the horse too much to deal with at the one time. When the horse is going through training we almost always ride them with and without a bit simply because it makes them more complete and gives the owner a choice in where they want to go with their horse.

There are a few ways to get the horse used to something in their mouth i.e. metal, rubber, plastic or leather bit, to name just some. Simply putting your thumb in the corner of your horse's mouth can do wonders not only for bitting but also as good prep for vet examinations and worming them. Sometimes we will put some vet-wrap on either side of the mouthpiece to give the bit a softer feel for the horse, especially youngsters. You can prep with a lead rope, getting them used to putting it in and out of their mouths till they are calm.

Once the bit is in you can do some short longlining session to get them use to the feel and action of the bit, this also applies to bitless bridles.

If you're moving from bit to bitless or vice versa, take your time and let the horse find their way to what you're looking for. Hopefully, if you are patient and sympathetic enough your horse will always know that you will let them think their way back to you and then both human and horse can continue their journey on the path of least resistance.

This method of putting the bridle on looks for the horse to yield to pressure and lower their head into position allowing the handler to slide the reins over the horse's head in preparation for putting the bit in.

NOTE: In this position you are not having to wrestle with the horse's head above your own.

Once the bit is in the handler will take great care in placing the horse's ears through the head piece ensuring the brow band is adjusted for comfort.

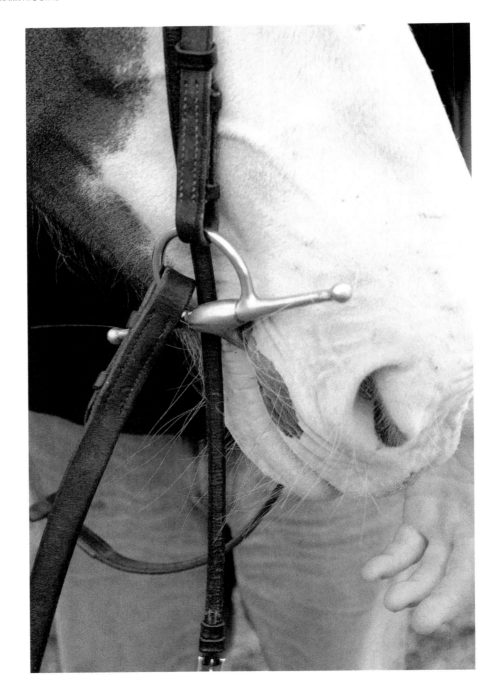

"A goal is not meant to be reached,
it often serves simply as something to aim at."
Unkown

Now the bridle is on all that remains is for the throatlash to be fastened.

Long lines

Double lines or Doppler Longe, working a horse with two lines has a few different titles but the training is similar. In our system we tend to long line primarily youngsters, remedial horses or horses coming off an injury. We have three different styles that we use; the first is simply attaching the lines to the halter with no roller.

We would like to reiterate that unless your horse had done plenty of good groundwork (especially line work) that it would be inadvisable to go straight to long lining as your horse may not be prepared well enough to cope with this.

When we start a horse in long lining, we keep the equipment as simple as possible; this benefits the horse as there is less pressure on them. In the picture above the horse is wearing a simple web halter with long lines.

"I have never known a strong person with an easy past."
Unkown

Here you can see the line has been thrown out. We can do this safely because we have already exposed the horse to lines on the ground and we are preparing to attach the second line to the offside of the halter.

The handler has the attached line over his arm and should the situation arise, where he needs to take charge of the horse he can do so quickly and easily.

"I didn't change. I just see things differently now."
Unknown

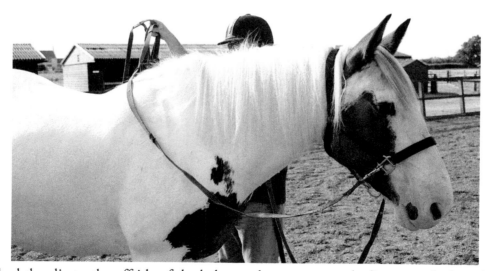

We have attached the clip to the offside of the halter and now we pass the line over the horse's neck where it will rest over the horse's withers.

In the above pictures the handler has now thrown the second line out and will pause for a moment to ensure the horse is still ok with this before proceeding.

If the horse is ok then we can move the line down over the quarters and look for the horse to stand in position.

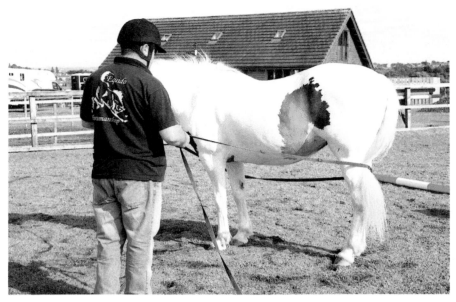

In the next sequence of photographs the handler asks the horse to move off. If the horse gets confused then the handler can apply a light contact on the outside rein to back up the initial prompt.

The next sequence of photographs shows the horse walking out confidently.

Once the horse is moving confidently the handler will initiate a change of rein which will loop the horse back to the marker C.

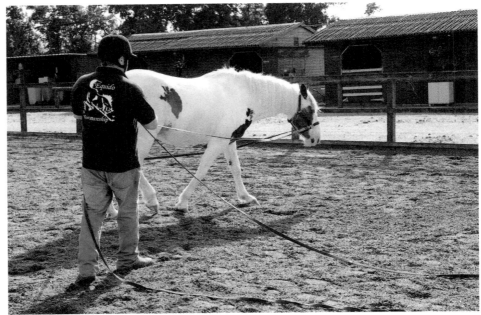

The next request the handler will make is for a halt. Once the horse is standing still the handler will approach the horse and remove the lines as shown in the following sequence of photographs.

As you can see in the top photograph the handler has dropped the line. The horse has already been prepared during the single line work to be comfortable with standing with the line on the ground.

Standing by the horse's head we would start to coil the line in and again, looking at the horse's expression you can see she is very comfortable with this.

Long Lining with Tack

Now the saddle and bridle have been introduced we can clip the lines onto the bit.

You can carry both lines in your hands but we prefer to clip one line onto our belt loop, this leaves both hands free to attach the stirrup hobble.

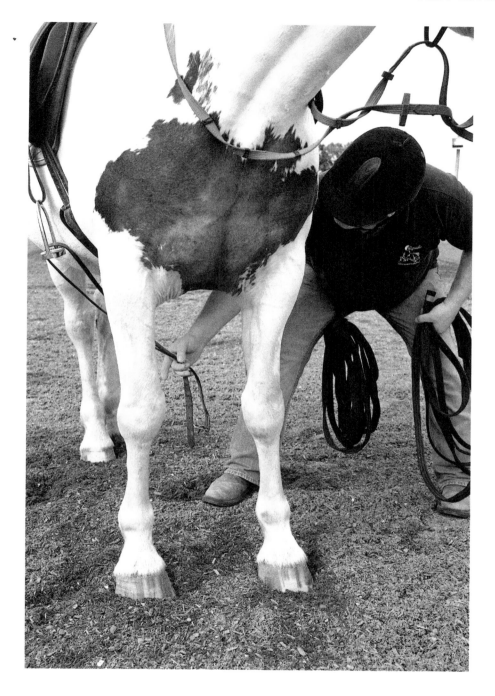

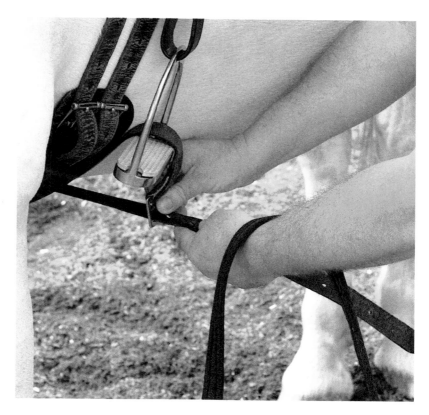

"A quiet mind is all you need.
All else will happen rightly, once your mind is quiet."
Sri Nisargadatta Mahara

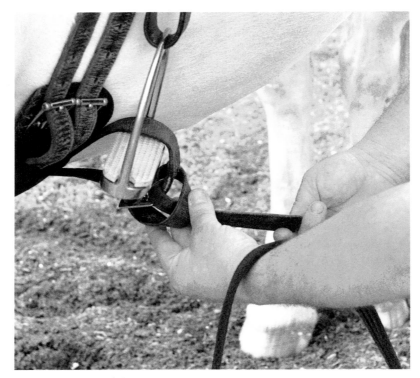

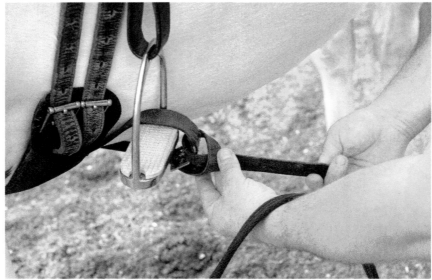

The handler has already attached one line and is now preparing to use the second line, which is passed over the seat of the saddle.

"Always have an option."
Mark Rashid

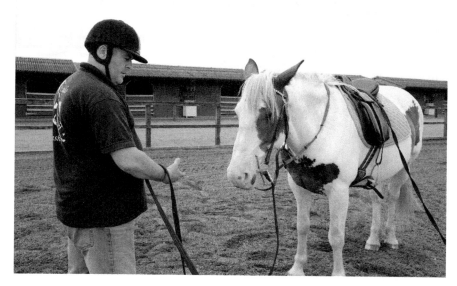

Keeping the attached line draped over one arm (the line can be dropped instantly should an emergency occur), the handler moves to the other side of the horse in preparation to attach the other line.

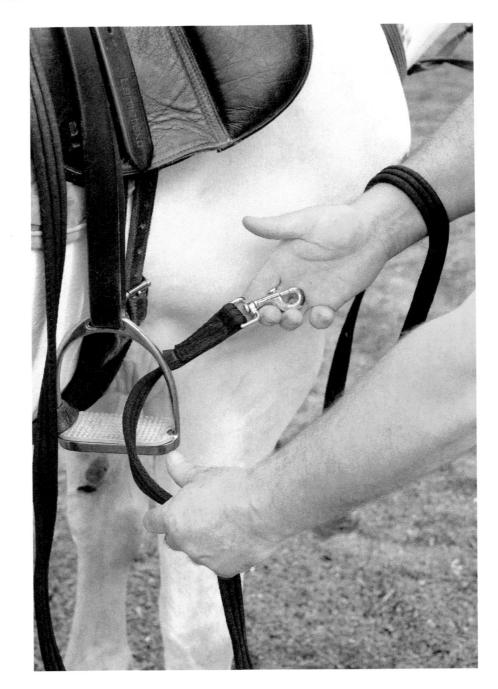

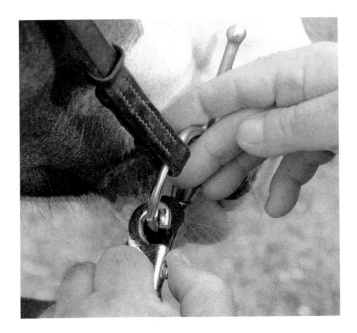

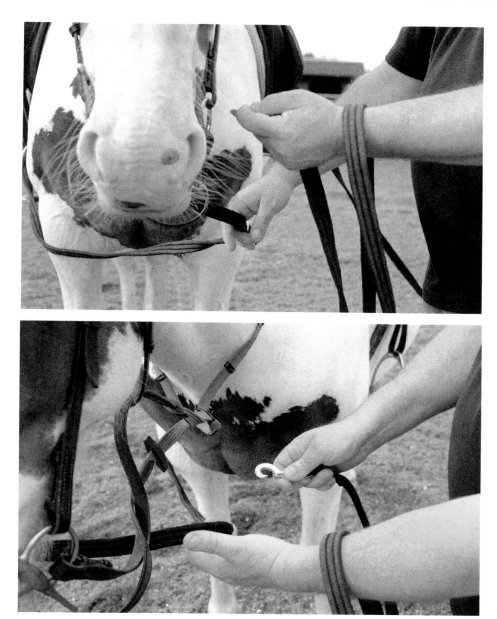

The handler returns to the left hand side of the horse, unclips the line from the bit, passes it through the stirrup and re-attaches it to the bit.

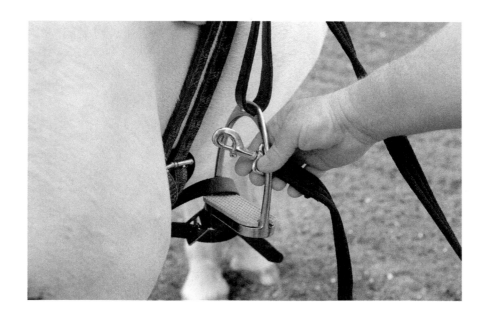

As with long lining without a saddle, we slid the offside line down over the horse's quarters and look for the horse to remain standing in position.

The horse now moves off and again we would look for a series of changes of rein, stops and circles.

In the lower photograph the handler is exaggerating how we would use our hands and arms as 'shock absorbers' so that there is no harsh contact on the bit.

"The world is round, anything you're running away from you are actually running towards."
Mark Higgins

*"Every accomplishment starts
with the decision to try."*
John F Kennedy

In the above photographs and the following two images we can clearly see how the handler holds the lines. Please note in the close up photographs the handler can initiate a halt simply by closing his hands on the line.

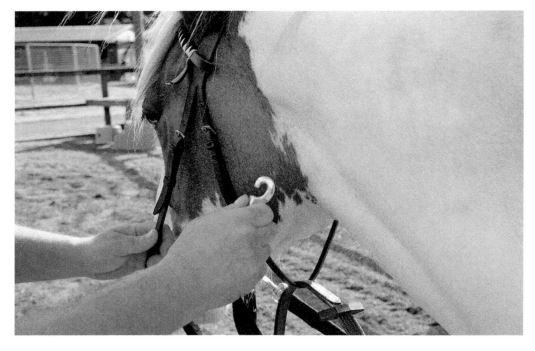

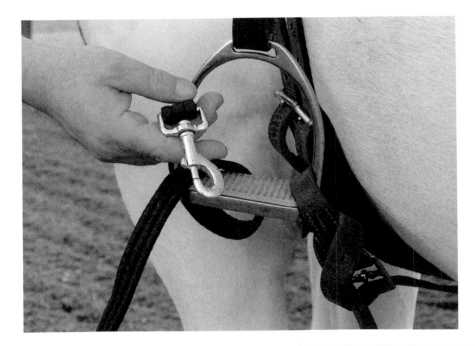

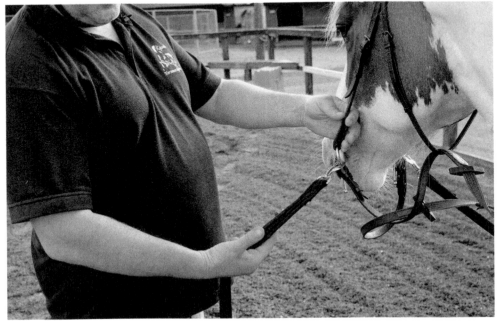

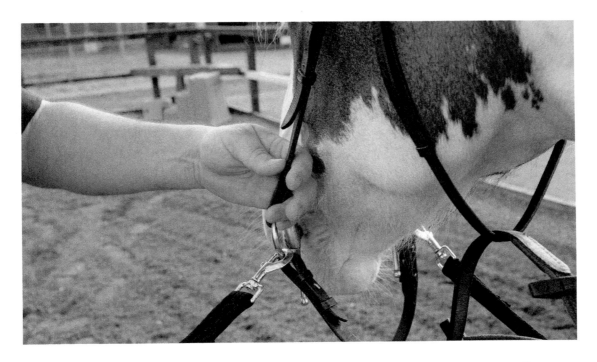

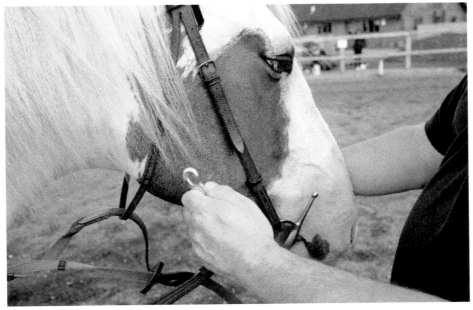

Once the handler has completed the final halt, he looks for the horse to stand in position while he removes the long lines.

NOTE: When the handler removes the lines he always maintains a point of contact with the horse

This is a very good way to start young horses and make them more familiar with things around them and stopping with an even contact on both sides. The next style is used when the tack is on, which is the style most people are familiar with, in this set up the lines are attached to the bit and run through the stirrups then sit around the hind quarters. In the final step again the lines are attached to the bit and run through the stirrups but this time we have attached two clips to the D rings on the pommel of the saddle which changes the angle of contact we have with the horse and allows us to work them in a better outline.

Working a horse on lines has so many benefits for us and the horse's we work with, it allows us to see how the horse is working and also gives us a better viewpoint to any issues that we need to address in the ridden work. For young horses it gets them exposed to the feel of the bit and also the feeling of contact on both sides that eventually will be replaced with the rider's legs.

With troubled horses it is a safer way to direct the movement of the horse if there have been problems with the riding aspect of their education, and of course at this point we will have ruled out any physical issues by giving the horse a complete veterinary check including x-rays if necessary.

Long reining, is very similar to longlining but you are in more direct contact with the horse usually behind either side of the hind quarters, sometimes touching them, the contact is held higher thus allowing the handler to achieve elevated paces and movement. We don't practice this style much but we do look for the same level of skill from horseback.

Chapter Seven - Liberty Work

Working a horse at liberty, to those who do not know this term, is moving the horse without any physical attachments. You can simple use your body position to do this or you may have to prompt the horse using a line, lunge whip or flag stick. Ideally we want to just use our body position when working the horse, this goes back to the concept of our bodies actions meaning something to the horse, but in the early stages of training we may have to prompt and usually a line will get the job done.

We only use liberty work to see where we are with our horse's focus or if we want to loose school a young horse that needs work on balancing their paces.

For us there is no practical application for liberty work other than what we have already discussed or maybe show or movie work. We see **a lot** of shut down horses that are nothing more than robots. When there is not a lot of horse left inside it moves away from horse training to horse draining. That being said not all liberty trainers switch their horses off but what we do see is people trying to use these concepts and getting lost and it is always at the horse's expense. Leave the tricks to the performers.

This is the starting position. In this opening photograph (top left) the handler has put on a white shirt and hat to allow you to better see the positioning. A lot of the liberty work will mirror the work carried out on single and double line work i.e. turn, changes of rein across the work area etc.

Here the handler is moving the horse out and beginning the training session.

In the bottom photograph the handler has dropped further back on the quarters, which has left a space for the horse's nose to fall into. In the pictures opposite he has corrected this by simply moving further up the horse's body which directs her out onto the fence line.

As we have seen in previous photographs if we drop further back on the horse it will cause the nose to tip into the inside. We now utilise this to initiate a circle as can be seen by the following sequence of photographs.

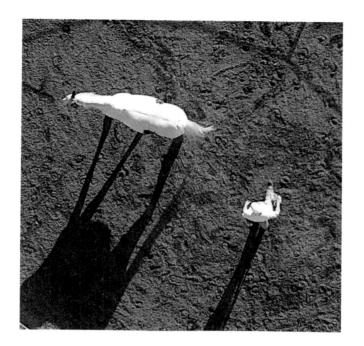

If the handler wants to initiate a change of rein through the centre of the round pen he would start in a similar fashion to the circle.

Around halfway through the circle the handler will walk parallel with the horse which will direct her into the other direction.

Once the handler has completed another circuit or two he will ask the horse to execute a small turn on this rein, then he would ask for another change of rein as we would like to keep the work programme balanced.

The handler simply stops in the middle and invites the horse in to finish. Sometimes the horse will come right up to the handler but on other occasions the horse will turn in but maintain a distance. As this is a shared experience between the handler and horse it is at this point that we may have to move to the horse to finish the exercise.

Again it is always important to remember to finish on a good note.

Chapter Eight - Loading

At some point we will want to move our horse, whether it's to a show, change of yard or a trip to the vets. You may have bought your horse and he was transported to the yard by the sellers and allegedly got on fine and traveled well. One thing we have learned over the years is 'never assume'. Just because your horse came to you alright doesn't mean he was happy about the experience. Horses by nature don't like tight spaces, one of the things you'll hear quite a bit of is 'my horse loves his stable', no, your horse tolerates his stable. And the same applies to traveling, horses tolerate the experience but they don't love it. Just like us going on holiday we may not like flying but we tolerate being stuck on a plane with hundreds of other passengers.

We feel it is the owner's responsibility to make the traveling experience for the horse as good as it can be. We have a duty of care to this animal or animals and for us this is of paramount importance. If we have been diligent in our groundwork there should not be too many issues, but there are always going to be horses that have a negative association with boxes/trailers that has to be worked through.

Usually when you have a horse that has a deeper issue with loading we need to be very clear in our direction and often things can get quite animated in the process of change. Getting your horse to move off of pressure and your timing and intent will help to assist this process of learning.

We'll give you an example of this application. We had been asked to go to Glasgow University VET School to load a horse that had been in for treatment and needed to go home. The owner and some of the vets and vet students had tried to load the horse several times with no success; they even sedated the horse in an attempt to push her on, all to no avail. They had been trying on and off for two days when we got the call, so we said we'd come and have a look and see if we could get things moving on.

The area to work in was not that great but we gave it a go. For about 30/40 minutes we tried to find out where the horse was and what had been done to her. She was pretty defensive and well versed at avoiding key areas at the horse box ramp but we worked away to see if she would come around and settle, she didn't. At this point we made the decision to take complete control of everything; we changed her headcollar to a pressure halter and just moved her around, this time on my terms. Usually when we decide to do this it is because the horse is on the verge of switching to survival mode so before this happens we prefer to take charge for the benefit of all concerned, especially me. By giving her strict direction she was on the box in five minutes and eating her hay, job done.

Ideally we want to train our horses to load. Like most aspects of training if you do it sympathetically its there for life, all you have to do then is work on refining it. There are other times however, like we have discussed above, where the situation is more about the safety of the handler and the handler taking charge of the situation for the benefit of the horse. Most of the time a horse has negative issues with traveling because their first exposure to it was unsympathetic, for some their self preservation instinct overwrites whatever training they may have had. Another aspect we should consider, has the horse been involved in some sort of accident?

What is important to remember when starting to prepare your horse for loading is the groundwork. Give your horse the chance to experience situations that they may encounter in the box or trailer in a less intimidating environment. Make sure they are comfortable with small spaces and unusual surfaces before approaching the box or trailer.

Here we have set up a plastic pole and jump wings against the arena fence. When the handler starts this exercise the gap between the pole and the fence is wide allowing

the horse to become familiar with the task. The handler would gradually close the gap until it is just wider than the horse, this mimics the spacing in a trailer.

We can also send the horse through the gap instead of leading her.

Here the handler has put a simple water tray in the gap to allow the horse to become familiar with unusual surfaces.

Our goal is to be able to allow the horse to almost self load. Once the horse is comfortable with the previous exercise we would move on to sending the horse through the gap with the handler on the outside.

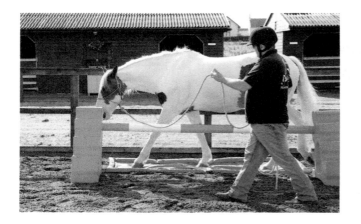
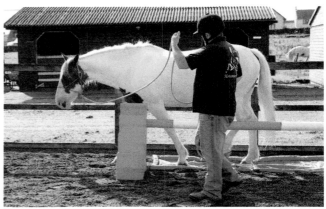

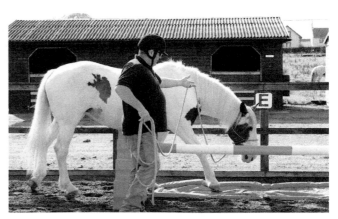

Having practised this a few times on both sides the handler would now move on to a different exercise.

The handler takes the driving exercise to the next stage which is sending the horse through the gap at a distance.

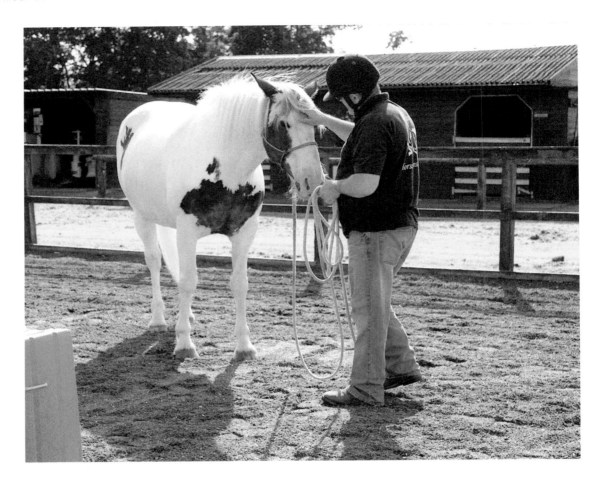

Finish the work on a good note.

NOTE: When practising these exercises, allow yourself to become familiar with them, we would advise that you use a horse that is comfortable working with you.

"Happiness is an inside job.
Don't assign anyone else that much power over your life."
Unknown

The handler has placed the horsebox in a safe environment for this training. Take time to allow your horse to investigate, they are inherently nosey and we want to use this to our advantage and not rush the horse in any way.

NOTE: We have removed the partition from the box and we can remove the breast bar if necessary. This helps to set the horse up to succeed.

The handler has stepped to the side to allow the horse plenty of time and space to explore.

NOTE: We always have a hay net inside the box, remember it is up to the horse to make the decision if they want to eat from it. A horse that is stressed will be less likely to eat from the net.

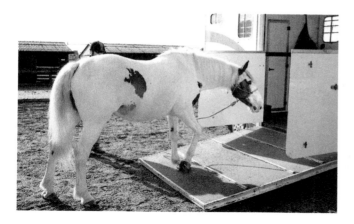

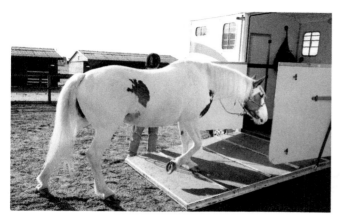

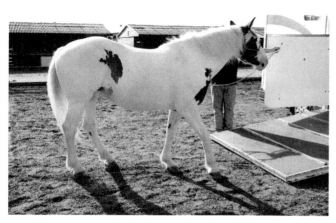

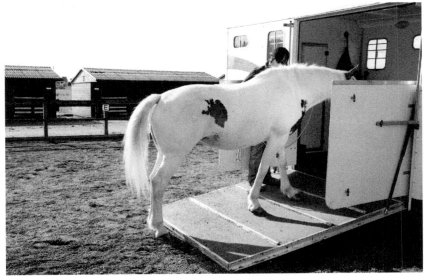

Here the horse has made the decision to go onto the box and the handler is simply supporting her and in a good position to assist if necessary.

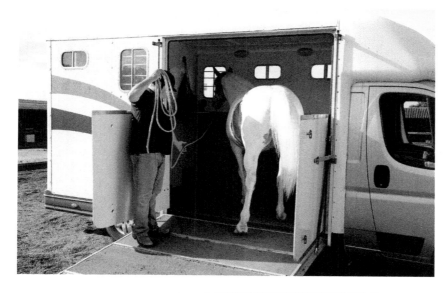

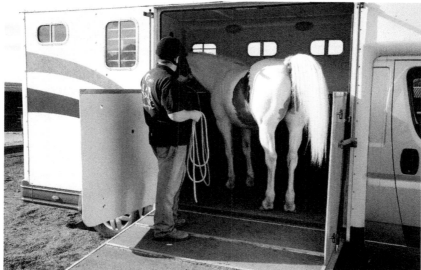

If your horse does a dropping in the box leave the droppings as this allows the space to feel and smell familiar to the horse.

Sometimes you may be working with a horse that has small feet and we have found that putting a small piece of wood in the gap at the top of the ramp helps to prevent the horse from getting their feet jammed. This is just another way of helping the horse to get things right.

NOTE: Please remember to remove the wood before trying to raise the ramp.

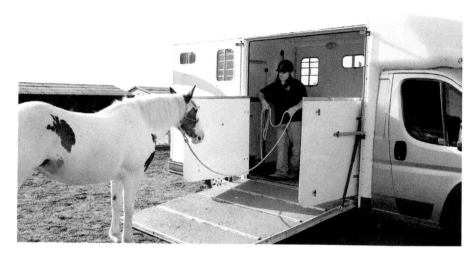

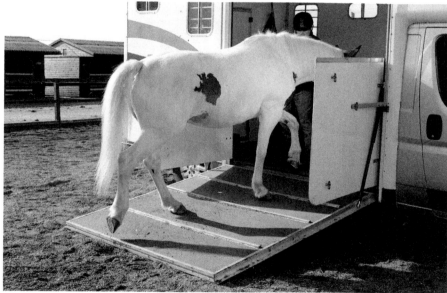

There are some trainers that feel that a horse should not be led onto the box, however, we feel that it is our job to do what is comfortable for the horse. Our goal is to send the horse onto the box but initially we may have to lead them on.

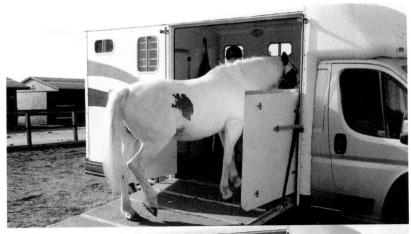

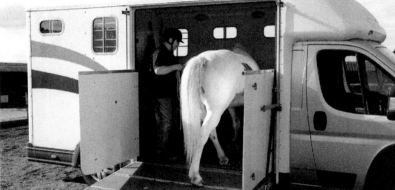

Although this is slightly a different method of loading the end results are the same.

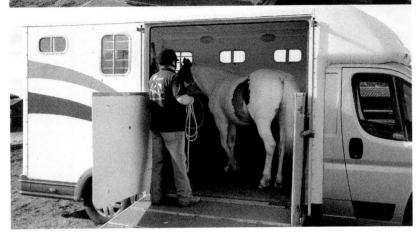

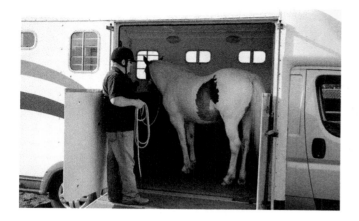
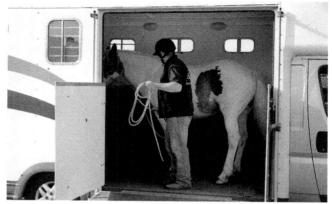
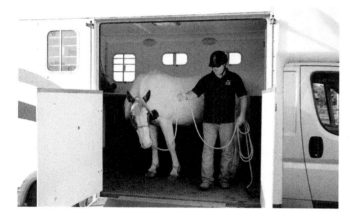
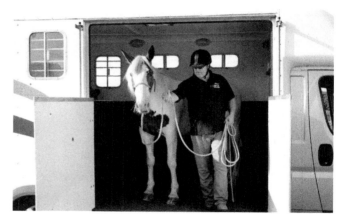

Once the handler has the horse loading nicely they would focus on making sure the horse does not rush coming off.

It is always good practise to train your horse to be able to load from different angles.

One of the goals when working with a horse who may be evasive, is that the handler must always make the centre point of the ramp a quiet space. If there is any movement away from this area then the horse would be re-directed back to that quiet spot.

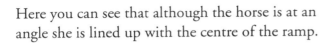

Here you can see that although the horse is at an angle she is lined up with the centre of the ramp.

Here is an internal view of the horse self-loading. ***Brave camera work!***

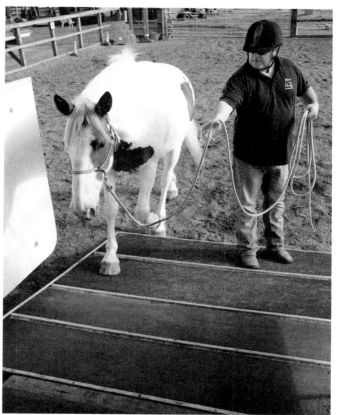

"Don't be afraid to fail, be afraid not to try."
Unknown

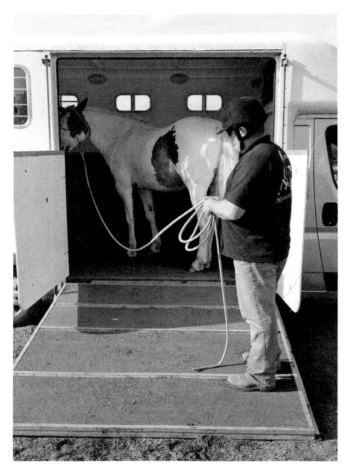 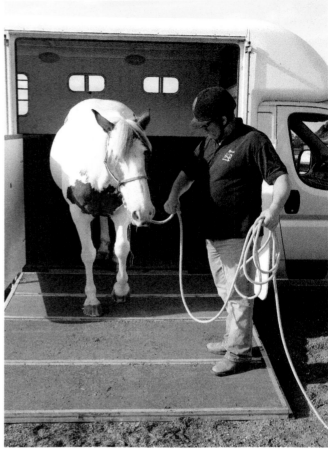

Once you have the horse loading and unloading confidently, it is useful to work on being able to halt the horse at any point when she is coming down the ramp. The handler may even back the horse up the ramp and into the box again.

NOTE: This is particularly relevant for loading horses onto trailers, even front off loaders as there may be times, due to damage, where the horse may have to be taken off or on backwards.

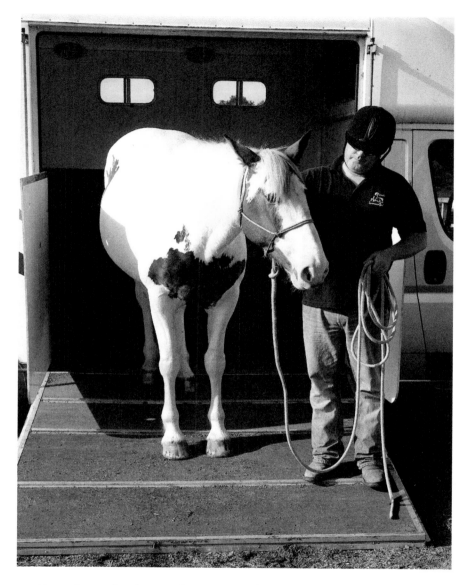

Here is the horse standing nice and calm on the ramp with the handler.

Chapter Nine - Finding Solutions

Usually you get to this section of training books and it's called 'trouble shooting' or 'problem horses'. These titles are fine but there is a tone in the wording. We chose finding solution because it fits better with how we think about a horse, and it sits nicely with the approach we would use for any issues they may have.

A common misconception is that there is an issue with the horse, when usually it's the other way around. One of the reasons for this is simply the handler/rider is inexperienced and isn't in a position where they can think their way around potential situations that may arise.

One of the things we say to people is, there are some horses that the whole ridden thing is a no-go area and that may be for physical reasons or a mental block or trauma. This is a tricky subject especially for owners who have may have been a bit naive when purchasing their horse and have paid out, sometimes, a fair bit of money and may not have bothered getting the horse vetted. You can only help a horse that wants help or is at the point of change, likewise with the human. That being said we do encourage the horse owner to be actively involved in the training or re-training of their horse, we are out to help both parties. Most of the time with the horse/human relationship the human is doing too much or not enough and the horse is trying to fill the gaps the only way they know how.

Horses are prey animals and usually deal with things in a couple of ways, they run, they freeze or they fight, but there is something else that is a big part of most horse's makeup, they are curious. We call this the nosey gene and we can use it to help horses with some of the issues that may pop up in our interactions with them.

Catching

Before we do anything with the horse we have to bring them in from grazing. This can be such a big deal for people, they tend to focus on the 'not being caught' part and less on the 'why'. The 'why' part can be a multitude of different reasons, something simple like, every time you catch your horse you overwork it in the school then throw the poor horse back into the field without any cool down or thanks. Very quickly the horse will associate the human with unpleasant work and this can lead to catching issues. Other times the horse may be carrying an old injury and is doing what it would do in the wild with a predator around. Often in these situations a horse will keep the injured side away from you and only present you its strong side. This can make you get out of position and can put you in the drive area and inadvertently make you keep pushing the horse away.

The above are just a couple of examples of possible causes for the horse to move away from you, there are others such as trauma or the horse is young and no one took the time to teach the horse that we are a good place to be. Being a good place to be or a reliable herd member is key to most, if not all, issues with your horse. We have to be the place of least resistance. If your horse is hard to approach or nervous to catch, a good starting point is using similar positioning as seen earlier in the liberty work section. The most common mistake that people make with their horses when faced with this situation is that as the horse walks away the human falls directly behind the horse and ends up in a direct driving position. If we look at the liberty work there are a lot of curved lines rather than straight lines, this can encourage the horse to turn toward you rather than moving away from you. This is a skill that takes time to become fluent in.

Haltering your horse, now that your horse will come to you in the field you must if you can make a more physical connection that will allow you to move on with your relationship and that will hopefully educate you both.

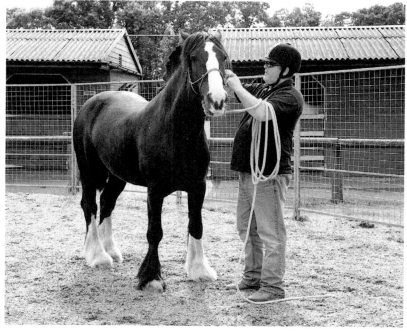

Your horse may have a bit of trust in you, but like most things in the early stages it can be easy lost. Before the halter goes on get the horse comfortable, rub them all over especially around their neck and head. If they are okay with your approach you can quickly gauge where they are mentally. There is **NO** point in try to halter a horse that isn't ready, your better doing good work and not getting the halter on than rushing things and wasting all your good work including the catching aspect, we are looking for **TRUST.**

Ideally we look for the horse to lower their head down to the halter, we can assist them in this by gently asking them to drop their head with light pressure to the crest or poll with an open hand, it's important that you don't dig your fingers in or ask too firmly which will cause the horse to brace or, at worst, run. Once your horse is comfortable lowering their head to the halter slip it on, being careful not to spook them with the head piece, and if they are comfortable then go ahead and buckle the halter up. There are a couple of ways to do this as you can see from the pictures.

Boundaries or lack of

As we have discussed earlier, boundaries are necessary for both you and your horse. Usually our boundary is initially at arms length but we can change that distance quite simply by bending our fingers, wrist, elbow or dropping our whole arm. Also we can make it as big as necessary depending on our horse's response, we can send the horse to the end of a longline if they are needing some room to work things out.

As you can see from this picture the horse is waiting for the handler to invite her in. At the moment the handler is talking to the spectators.

Mounting block, we see so many people make this simple thing, getting on their horse, a very difficult concept for the horse to grasp. The most common thing we have noticed is the mounting block moves more than the horse. Secondly, and one of our biggest irks, the horse moves then the rider executes a superman like leap onto the horse. The horse gets a fright, the rider gets thrown and it's all the horse's fault.

The biggest focus for our work is setting things up so the horse and the human succeed, again breaking things down into there constituent parts will help us greatly. Be patient, keep your emotions in neutral; it may take as much time to get things where they should be as it did for them to get out of sync in the first place. Your groundwork will help you and it would be a good idea to start with no tack on (as shown previously) and build things up from there. Most of this work is about stripping back the layers then overlaying a more complete picture for you and your horse.

There are many reasons for a horse losing confidence at the mounting block i.e. poor handling, pain associated with the tack and rider, lack of training or the horse has always been mounted from the ground or rider legged up.

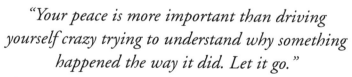

If the issue is caused by pain then you must have your saddler, vet, body worker, address the issues.

If it is an issue caused by improper handling then we would approach the horse's training in the same fashion as we would do for a horse being started under saddle.

With a horse that might have had a negative experience at the mounting block, we have to overlay the negative experience with a more positive one. Basically we are re-mapping the area on and around the mounting block.

"Your peace is more important than driving yourself crazy trying to understand why something happened the way it did. Let it go."
Garui de Guzman

Once the horse is more familiar with the area around the mounting block and is comfortable being there, we can start looking for more precision in the placement of the feet. In doing this we are asking the horse to position themselves in a place that is beneficial for the rider to mount them.

If this is done correctly the horse will eventually move up into the correct position of their own accord. Allowing the rider to mount, adjust stirrups or girth with the reins remaining at the buckle safe in the knowledge that the horse will not try to walk away.

Usually when the handler is working on these types of issues, they would adjust the stirrups, lean over the horse, move the saddle etc and check that the horse is ok with the tack being moved around.

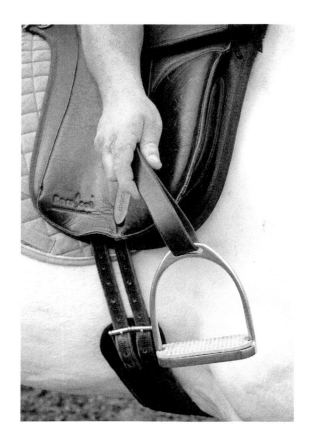

"Don't be afraid to make mistakes. Being human can be great.
No matter what is on your plate, be grateful."
Unknown

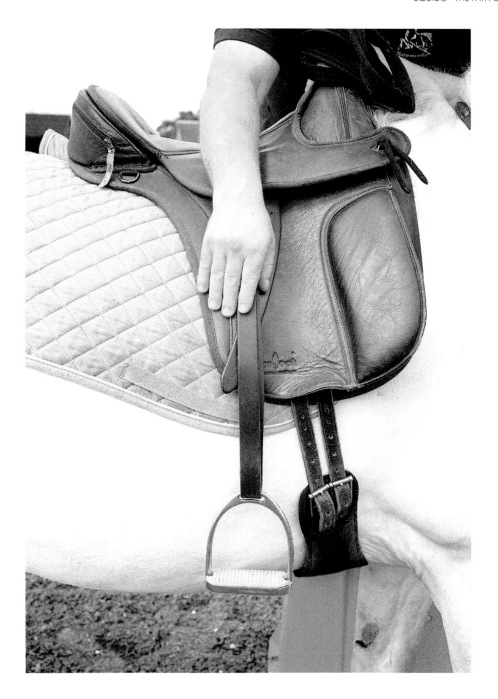

You can see that the horse is really relaxed standing at the block, remember to always finish on a good note.

Unfamiliar Surfaces

Have you ever been out at a pond with your friends on a cold winter's morning and decided to play on the ice. So off you go, then you hear a cracking sound (almost every person on the planet who has heard that noise will freeze if you pardon the pun). This is how we as humans respond to a potential threat. The next thing that happens is that you start thinking about getting off the ice as quickly and safely as possible. This is the second response to danger, run. If we are unlucky and the ice breaks then we quickly move on to the third response, fight, in this case as in any other life-threatening situation we are fighting for our lives. Now these responses can come in any order and they are hard wired into our self-protection systems, live, breed, the species continues to evolve.

Horses have the same survival mechanisms as we do. They tend to be slightly more heightened than ours as most prey animals are. Most horses are extremely careful when it comes to their legs, their legs are, a mode of transportation, used for survival and to a big degree a sensory appendage, needless to say they tend to be very aware of where they will put them. We need to work with the horse when we present new things to them, especially if it is something they are going to walk over. We usually use a tarp, heavy plastic sheet or stable mat in our work with the horse, most of which is to prep for loading. However you can use it as a simple exercise in trust building.

When working with the horse always work on the curious side of their nature, if they want to smell the object then let them do so, if they paw it let them do so, this is normal horse behaviour. When they sniff and paw it's their way of assessing what the object is and if it's safe to stand on. Our part of this process is facilitating the change from curiosity to action, now this is a skill in itself but as we have discussed previously if we set it up correctly then there is a good chance that we horse and human will achieve our goal. Once the horse is confident in you as someone who will do their very best never to put them in a dangerous position then they will go most places with you.

Nervous/dangerous horses, I've put these two types together as there is usually some confusion as to which is which. Sometimes when a horse has been handled in a negative way over a period of time they can present nervous aggressive behaviour which means that given the correct stimulus they shift very quickly into a fight mode of response. Some horses are born with a heightened fight instinct which could be treated by balancing out that chemical imbalance. These types of horses really need careful management, getting the horse on a tight regime of proper groundwork can help along with sympathetic handling that encourages positive behavioural responses that can lead to a safer environment for all.

Stallions, if not handled and managed properly, can be extremely dangerous to both humans and horses alike. In our opinion there is not enough control with regards to breeding and that's a global issue. Also, if you do not have the correct facilities where horses can live in family groups, then you shouldn't be breeding horses. We feel that it is cruel to have a stallion whose only purpose is to win rosettes and service the odd mare. It's not the stallions fault if someone gets hurt, he is working off hormones and instinct. So, get your horses gelded.

There are however some horses that are born with a mental defect. Usually Mother Nature would sort these horses out but in a domestic environment this does not always happen. Most of the time these types of horses don't even act like horses, the mother will tend to reject them and they end up being hand reared.

This horse was nervous and could be aggressive when pushed. He would throw his weight around, run off and kick out. The horse had never been shown a better way of being around humans. Because of his background he needed some very direct handling in the early stages and the handler had to use a flag anytime he was working around the back legs due to the horse's potential to kick out.

Here you see how the horse would kick out when the flag is introduced to the quarters area.

NOTE: In the photographs the horse's head is tipped towards the handler so that he can direct the hindquarters away from him.

"When you inspire yourself first, others are naturally inspired."
Sandi Amorim

In the above two photographs the horse is beginning to feel a bit better about himself and we decided to move on to something else.

Loading Issues

Sometimes when a horse has a mental block about a particular object e.g. horsebox, trailer, mounting block etc it can manifest as a physical brace. In these cases our goal is to unlock the horse both mentally and physically, which can, on occasions, get very animated. The horse in the next sequence of photographs is the same horse that was nervous/aggressive. He also had issues with the horsebox.

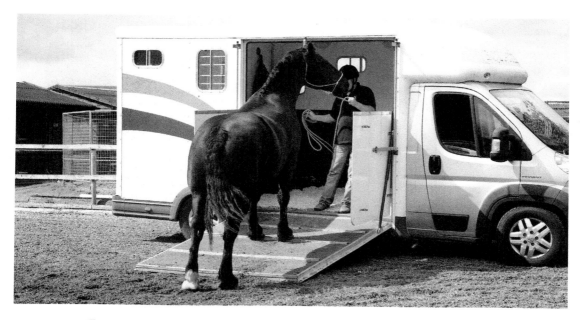

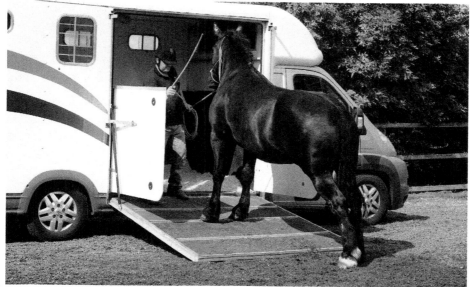

Our goal was to ask him on and just before he chose to leave we would make the decision to move away from the horsebox. This enabled us to maintain our ability to direct him in a more positive manner.

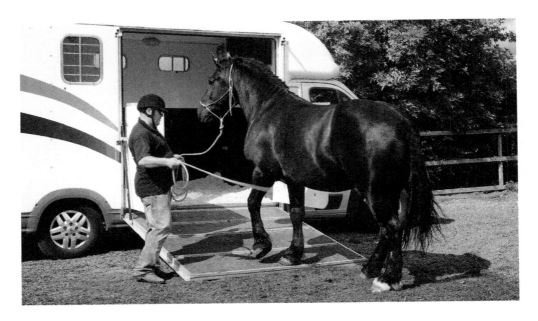

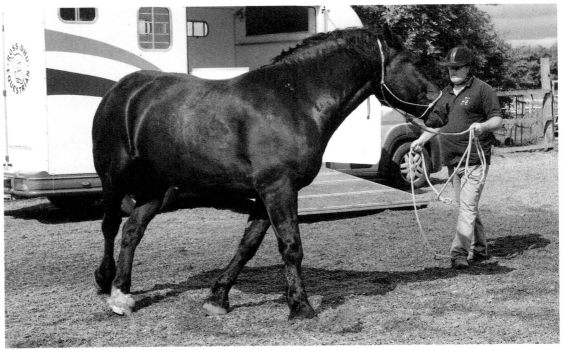

There is a lot of discussion back and forth between the handler and the horse and it can sometimes feel like there will be no breakthrough. At this point most people give up, when in fact they should actively continue with their task.

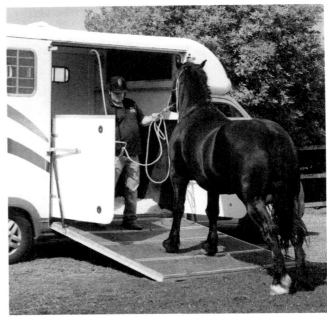
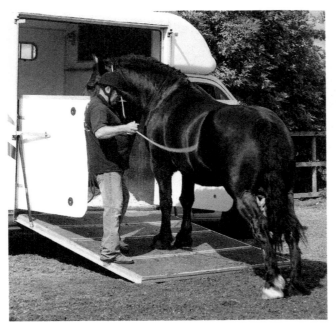

With perseverance the handler managed to successfully load the horse. Most people would think at this point that the horse can now load when in fact this is the start of his training.

As you can see from the photographs, this horse being a Percheron cross, found the box a bit of a tight squeeze. We have taken out the partition and the front bar whilst training to make it more comfortable for him and safer for the handler.

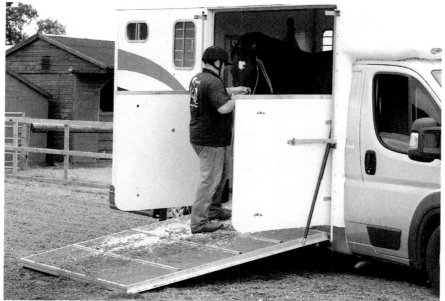

We found that once on he had a tendency to try to rush off. We simply redirected his energy back towards the ramp.

NOTE: You will **NEVER** stop a one tonne horse from moving, therefore always think of your safety first.

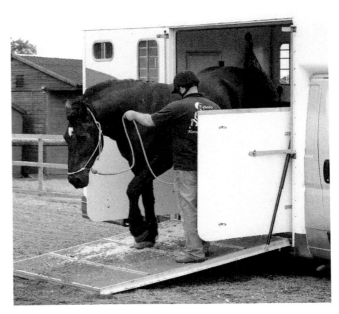
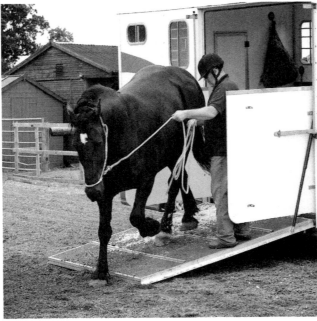

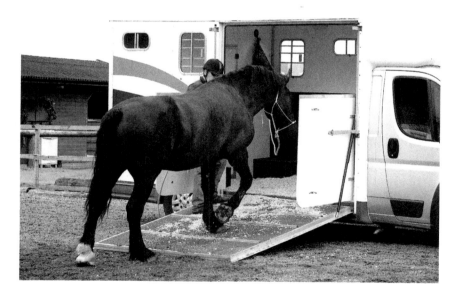

You can see in the photographs above, the handler redirects the horse back towards the box.

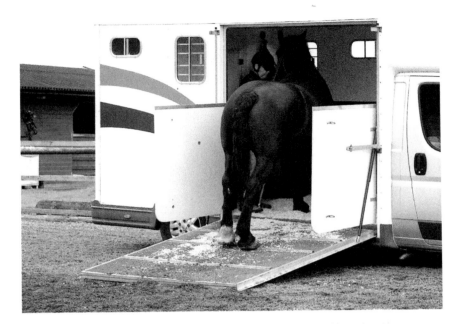

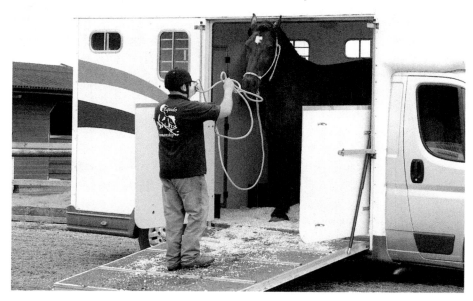

Having repeated this process a few times the horse became more comfortable staying in the box, so much so that we could now safely block him from rushing off and he would stand quietly.

In the above photographs you can see the handler asking the horse to stay in position inside the box before being asked to leave the box in a calmer manner.

It took several more sessions of loading before the horse became more settled. We are glad to say that he went home easily and is going from strength to strength.

Hand Rearing

This is a very skilful process, if done correctly the horse should grow up like a normal horse but if done incorrectly and over-humanized then it's a whole different ball game. Most of the time these type of horse won't find the correct stimulus from the human, the bigger they get the rougher the play so to speak. If you watch youngsters in a herd there is a point when they are growing up usually around one year-old that the baby year stops and they start to learn to function as a valuable member of the herd.

In the end if you have a horse that is overly aggressive around human and horses then in our opinion the kindest thing to do for that horse is to put it to sleep (euthanize). As trainers we have to look at the big picture, be sympathetic when teaching but also sometimes we have to be blunt, firstly for the sake of the human and secondly the horse. We will say again **'safety of humans outweighs the safety of the horse'** this statement will obviously ruffle some feathers but we have to be practical in our horsemanship.

There are hundreds, if not thousands of perfectly safe, good to ride horses in the world that are looking for a loving home but people keep going for these 'rescue horse' types that would keep us on our toes let alone someone with vastly less experience. For most of us, horses are for pleasure and are not a contact sport, we have to think of our safety and others, that's the bottom line but you can only give advice, its up to others to see the value in it.

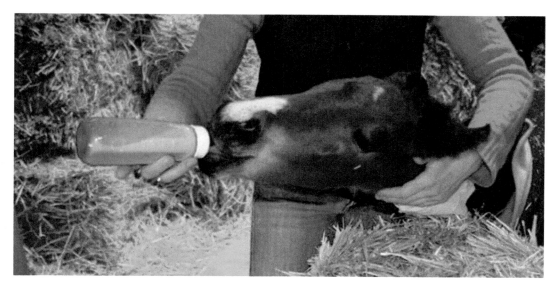

Chapter Ten - Something to Think About

Most people who work with horses for a living it is more of a lifestyle choice than a job. The diagram below represents a Japanese concept known as Ikigai which loosely translates as 'a reason for being'. In this concept everyone has Ikigai no matter what their walk of life is and this concept focuses more on a journey of self-discovery. It is similar to the French term 'raison d'etre' which means reason for being. We feel that this diagram best illustrates how, for us as trainers, our lives revolve around horses.

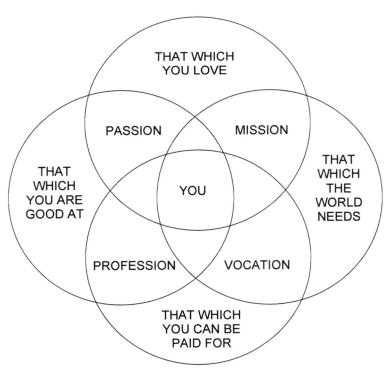

Conclusion

We have talked about many different areas of horsemanship, language, bodywork, assessing ourselves and the horse, groundwork and any issues that may arise. There has been a common thread linking all of these, our choice to look for better, more sympathetic ways to work and be with our horses. Our search for better ways to be with our equine partners should not become static or fixed; we should be in a constant state of refinement and renewal.

The aim in producing this book is to give people simple tools that can help them in their horsemanship. We have focused on keeping things clear and easy to follow which we hope will be beneficial to those who read it. There are many systems out there that are technique oriented where the horse ends up nothing more than an automated robot performing a series of pre-set responses. When a training system takes away the horse's spirit then it shifts from focusing on partnership to becoming a dictatorship, this does not sit easy with us. We look for our horses to be alert and responsive, not to just be a thing that does our bidding unquestionably.

Horsemanship doesn't have to be complicated; in fact the exact opposite could be said. We look to keep things simple by being transparent in all our interactions with our equine friends, partners, and family.

Our goal, for all horse owners, is that they enjoy the majesty of these wonderful, intelligent beings and for all those who stumble across this book we sincerely wish it leads you down a different road. Hopefully one day soon we will meet you on the path of least resistance.

"To do something with soul, creativity or love;
leaving a piece of yourself into what you are doing."
Meraki

"Riding a horse is not a gentle hobby, to be picked up and laid down like a game of solitaire. It is a grand passion. It seizes a person whole and once it has done so, you will have to accept that your life will be radically changed."
Ralph Waldo Emerson

"No one saves us but ourselves.
No one can and no one may.
We ourselves must walk the path."
Buddha

SUGGESTED READING AND WEBSITES

Any books by Mark Rashid

Buck Brannaman – The Faraway Horses

Dr Gerd Heuschmann – Tug Of War and Balancing Act

Tom Dorrance – True Unity

Bill Dorrance – True Horsemanship through Feel

www.equidohorsemanship.co.uk

www.scottishhorsehelp.co.uk

www.keeganphotography.co.uk

www.skyviewvideo.co.uk

www.markrashid.com

www.buckbrannaman.com

www.mastersonmethod.com

www.heartlinehorsetraining.com

www.clydevetgroup.co.uk

CHARITIES

A special mention for the charities we support:-

Alex Freeborn from BackOutThere who help soldiers transition from military to civilian life.

Sophie Misfud from Step Together who help people in need of support across the UK to take positive action to change their lives and the lives of others through community volunteering.

DISCLAIMER

Due to the unpredictable nature of horses it is important that readers understand that Equido® Horsemanship Ltd cannot be held responsible for injuries to person/s or their horse/s whilst practising the techniques shown in this book.

We advise anyone who works with horses to wear safety equipment (hard hat, gloves, back protector and suitable foot wear).

Lightning Source UK Ltd.
Milton Keynes UK
UKOW07f0315170917
309336UK00006B/8/P